Contents

The authors would like to dedicate this book to Jacob, Joshua, Oliver and Christopher and to all students with whom we have had the pleasure of working on their independent studies, and without whom the writing of this book would not have been possible.

List of figures and tables

Figures

Tables

About the authors

Rosie Walker is Foundation Degree Partnership Co-ordinator and senior lecturer within the Centre for Early Childhood, Institute of Education at the University of Worcester. She has supervised many research projects with Foundation degree, BA and Top-up students as well as Master's students and is responsible for managing student practice-based experience. Rosie has been involved in research projects with students and has presented her work at EECERA and BECERA as well as publishing within peer-reviewed journals. Previously, she has managed two phase 1 children's centres and is a social worker by professional heritage. Rosie has worked in a variety of childcare settings including child protection teams, the National Society for the Prevention of Cruelty to Children (NSPCC) and has worked as a child protection trainer and Guardian ad Litem.

Carla Solvason is a senior lecturer within the Centre for Early Childhood, Institute of Education at the University of Worcester. Part of her role involves co-ordinating and managing student independent studies for the BA and Top-up degree and in developing research within the centre and institute. Carla teaches on the BA, Top-up, Postgraduate Certificate of Education (PGCE) and Master's programmes and is a research degree supervisor. Prior to lecturing, Carla worked as a researcher, a consultant for schools looking to create communication-rich environments and a primary school teacher. Carla has published work relating to student research, the team around the student, school culture, educational equality and social justice.

Acknowledgements

The authors would like to acknowledge the work of all the contributors to this text. We would especially like to thank Emily Beaven, Nikki Field, Leanne Taylor, Catherine Jackson, Harriet Wood and Samantha Price for allowing us to use their studies to illuminate the research journey. Our thanks must also go to Michael Reed for his unstinting help and support throughout the writing of the book. Thanks also to Miriam Davey and Jude Bowen at Sage Publications for giving us the opportunity to write the book and for their help and enthusiasm about the project. Thank you to Jean McNiff for contributing her time to help us with this book, and to Bethany Lock and Daniel King for their student view of the work.

Foreword

Jean McNiff

Few practices require greater commitment than early years, and few areas are more important for research. The old Jesuit adage of 'Give me a child until the age of seven ...' was always significant: many of the metaphors we live by are formed in our early years, and many mental habits firmly established, none more so, perhaps, than the way we think, our logics and epistemologies. All the more important, therefore, that early years practitioners should research their teaching and caring practices to show how they hold themselves accountable for their work with young children; that they explain how they tread lightly so as not to distort the potential of minds that are in the wonderful process of formation.

A new mind is a miracle. It is an entirely original entity, never before and never again to be replicated throughout all eternity. Each one of us is unique, irreplaceable and unrepeatable. We are each born with the capacity for an unlimited number of creative acts: we are infinitely powerful. We each come into the world as a new beginning, potentially enriching the world by the very fact that we are born (Arendt, 1958). Each one of us occupies our own spot, our allocated place on Earth, and it is our responsibility to use it well. How immense therefore the responsibility of teachers and carers who have the capacity and the political authority to influence those minds, to use their influence well and in the best interests of the emerging mind of the child.

The accounts in this book show how the practitioners involved do this. Further, each account shows how the practitioner accepts the responsibility of explaining how they hold themselves accountable for what they do. There is a nice commensurability here, for young children also are powerful researchers. They spend much of their lives asking 'Why?' and offering their provisional conclusions about how their world works, and how they make sense of their actions in relation to their social and natural world. We are born as action researchers, as people who wish to find ways of improving our learning, and using that learning to improve our practices in the world. Perhaps a main significance of early years research is found in this element of demonstrating accountability in processes of emergence.

The book contains accounts that show this process in action, celebrating the potentials of action research as an appropriate methodology for valuing and encouraging new beginnings. The idea of new beginnings implies a moral stance, a powerful theme of the book, for emergence itself is ethical, a feature of evolutionary form, a feature of new minds. The evolutionary form is in danger of distortion when power-constituted structures are imposed on it, and open minds are threatened by being forced into orthodoxies that do not value freedom of thought and action. How important, therefore, that practitioners research their practices using a form that is itself dynamic and evolutionary, that celebrates their capacity for originality of mind and the creation of knowledge; that shows the same process of emergence as the minds they are working with and are encouraging to flourish. Action research somehow mirrors the entire process of children and teachers enjoying the experience of learning together, and using their learning to create new futures. This idea requires the celebration of an open epistemology that sees possibilities in everything, especially in the relationships between people, and between those people and their different worlds.

Action research and early years practices go together, as naturally as the new day rising. This book is a celebration of new days. Early years research is a practice for creative thinking for new tomorrows; the book shows us how to do this, and is to be commended for anyone who wishes to find innovative ways to think and act for all new beginnings.

Reference

Arendt, H. (1958) *The Human Condition*. Chicago, IL: University of Chicago Press.

Introduction

The writers of this book have had the pleasure of working with many student practitioners over the years and see this text as a celebration of those students' achievements. In using examples of research projects carried out in a range of settings and by students from differing backgrounds we hope to demonstrate to our readers that anyone can carry out small-scale good quality research. The unique premise of this book is that we use real research by individuals studying on early years courses, from Foundation Degree to Bachelor's Degree in order to demonstrate and explore some key elements of 'good' research. We have found in the past that students lack confidence in the area of research and feel that it is 'beyond' them – we hope that this book goes some way towards proving that it is not. We hope that the use of real examples will help to demystify what tutors are looking for within a research project and will go some way towards interpreting and demonstrating some of the difficult terminology that is used when discussing research.

Within academic tradition research has held a somewhat elevated position which causes some student practitioners to struggle to see how it relates to them. Although there are many similarities between the critical reflective practice cycle and research, students tend to be intimidated by the very prospect of research and to see it as something foreign to their day-to-day practice (Solvason, 2010). As Solvason (2011: 33) points out, 'research plays a part in every aspect of your career path' and involves 'making a concerted effort to look into a topic'. Reflective practice which is inherent in early years practice teaches students to not only consider their own views, but to consider the views of others when working within early years teams, and it is important that we make clear that research is simply a more systematic way of approaching this. In this text we hope to prove that research is as useful and as accessible a tool as any other that students develop during their studies and that it is fundamental to good practice. Rinaldi (2005: 148) encourages us to stop viewing research as the 'privilege of the few (in universities and other designated places) to become the stance, the attitude with which teachers approach the sense and meaning of life'. Our student practitioners are members of a research active community, and as members of that community they need to explore ways of knowing, proving and improving. The student work included in the following chapters provides examples of just this.

It is because of our belief that we are all members of a research active community that we have chosen to explore these concepts with the help and support of our students, just as we would hope that our students explore areas of interest alongside their colleagues in settings. It is important that our research demonstrates research 'with' and not research 'on' participants and settings as our students are a part of the early years ideology that is created and perpetuated; they are not separate from it (McNiff, 2011). In other words, the research that you carry out is part of an ongoing process of quality which asks practitioners to consider their values, beliefs and personal strengths, and engage in a thoughtful and holistic view of practice and their own contribution to practice (Appleby and Andrews, 2012).

Because of this active involvement in the world of early years care and education we need to investigate our areas of interest using an approach to research that is beyond ethicality, but that embodies kindness, respect and humility (Pring, 2004). Within this text we explore how this can be difficult at times due to the troublesome nature of research and particularly when one has the sometimes conflicting roles of student, practitioner and researcher.

It is important that practitioner research takes an appreciative stance, building upon existing strengths and looking for areas of further development. These areas for improvement apply foremost to yourselves as developing professionals but also to the settings within which you practice, as conduits of quality early years practice. As such your own development and improvements in the setting are intertwined within your research. As students, research can enhance your knowledge, understanding and practice, and improve your employability prospects. Settings should be encouraged to embed a culture of research within their day-to-day practice, so that the quality of practice can be enhanced and developed continually in the light of new discoveries. Rather than being a rite of passage for students, research can become a meaningful undertaking which continues throughout your career, a skill that is central to early years practice and essential if we are to develop and improve practice for children and families.

For these reasons it is important to start with the purpose of the research, what you want to explore within a limited time frame and with limited resources, before beginning to consider what the best methods are to do this. The passion and sense of exploration and curiosity we hope to engender in children is important for us to hold on to as students and practitioners. As professionals we continue on a learning journey and it is important to remember that this continues throughout our working lives. Research is not a 'one off'. As students, you are most often part of the community that you are researching; this is why the purpose of what you are researching and how it benefits you and the setting is such an important starting place. Research is not solitary; as Pascal and Bertram (2012a) suggest it should be carried out in mutually beneficial partnership with others, for immediate use, and have a strong ethical base. This ethicality embodies far more than simply gaining permissions, but should really consider Stern's (2011) kind and sensitive approach in working with the setting, acknowledging potential power imbalances and pitfalls as part and parcel of the research.

The role of being an early years practitioner and researcher is inextricably linked and our underpinning belief is that research in this field should be rooted in praxeological values in being carried out with and not on settings. Pascal and Bertram (2012b: 485) have drawn our attention to a developing model of praxeological research which:

> At its heart is a process of critical self-evaluation, reflection and action (praxis) with the guiding purpose of advancing practice and supporting practitioners to develop a more profound understanding of their work, and, therefore, a more effective delivery of services to children and families.

excellen[t]

It should be carried out in real-world situations within the company of others: 'to discover why we do what we do' (Pascal and Bertram, 2012b: 485), for immediate use and have a strong ethical base. This does not only mean gaining permissions but in using Stern's (2011) virtuous and caring approach in joining with the setting, acknowledging potential power imbalances and pitfalls as part of the research and including of the voices of children and parents. Formosinho and Formosinho (2012: 602) discuss the principle of attachment, '*reflexive attached commitment*' which includes close and intense working with the research setting and its participants, and with yourself as the main 'instrument' and 'important inquiry tool' of the research being clearly integrated into your written submission to ensure rigour.

NOT easy to get-

So, how does this book 'work'?

The book draws on six studies from students who provide a reflective introduction to each study. This will contextualise the study and explain a little bit about the student practitioner who wrote the text, their background, their aims in carrying out the research and the significance of the particular focus area. In taking this approach, we have sought to model good practice in using the voices of those most closely involved in work-based inquiry. We have also sought positive examples from our colleagues' work to support the points that we make. This book is not intended as a critical appraisal of existing literature.

Each of the chapters that follow is built around sound examples of students' work that look at an element of research. Extracts are used as a starting point to explore and build on what the students exemplify in structuring their own research project. Sometimes the extracts are lengthy, allowing you to fully see their thought process and how their approach has developed. Following the relevant excerpt/s from the study there will be discussion about it; its strengths, what ideas can be taken from it, how it could be built upon and how it relates to other foci within the book. We work systematically through each of the primary elements of research, but this does not imply that all research projects must be presented in this way.

The studies chosen were all of high quality, but they are not held up as exemplars to be replicated, but rather as studies you will (as early years practitioners and social scientists) be able to relate to within your day-to-day practice. Each study covers an area of concern within early years practice and shows how the researchers have tackled this within a variety of settings. You will notice that although the references used by the students are shown in the body of the excerpts, full reference lists are not given at the end. This is because we do not wish the subject matter that the student is exploring to become a focus within this book. These topics are used outside of the context of the full study. We have not corrected the references the students have used so be aware that these may not always be accurate. It is important for you, as researchers, to build up your own body of theory and references. The aim of the book is not to 'spoon-feed' anyone in terms of undertaking research, but to support you in understanding how to engage with this important strand of your practice and academic work, and to get a tangible idea of how sound research might 'look'.

The book is written by two authors who have each written chapters. Therefore, you may see some differences in style between the chapters, although we have worked closely together to make sure that our approach is consistent.

This text aims to empower you as students by using the work of peers and acknowledges that doing research can be a struggle. It will draw out issues of reflective practice by posing points for reflection, including questions and dilemmas during commentary on the studies. The book aims to offer the type of advice given in research tutorials, using real small-scale studies as examples of good practice and drawing out key learning points from these.

The studies

Samantha

Sam is currently the manager of a busy nursery within a rural area. At the time of undertaking the study she was a Foundation Degree student. She has considered practice at the setting in terms of literacy. Sam's motivation and concern on discovering that parents at her setting wanted more development of their children's literacy skills led her to formulate a tool for impacting on quality through her action research project. This is considered more fully in Chapter 2.

Emily

Emily is a family support worker in a children's centre in a large town set within a rural locality. She was a Foundation degree student at the time of the research and was concerned to explore the potential effects of proposed budget reduction for the centre on practitioners and ultimately how this would affect children and families. In view of the potentially sensitive nature of this study, Emily gave careful thought to ethicality, and this is discussed in Chapter 3.

Leanne

Leanne was a BA student at the time of writing and had 15 years' experience as a teaching assistant. She chose to research into how much time should be spent in adult-led and how much in child led activities within a reception class. She has taken a new innovative direction, in that she has reflected after each section of her study. This has been highly effective in helping the reader to understand her thought process and how her learning at each stage has been integrated into the research process. You can see this clearly with the literature review in Chapter 4.

Nikki

Nikki was a family support worker in a busy urban children's centre while undertaking her BA Top-up degree in Early Childhood Studies. At the time, her centre was concerned to develop partnership working with parents who would have an input into shaping services. She believes that the significance of the parent–child relationship should never be underestimated by any early years practitioner. Her passion for this area of work led her to analyse the existing practice at the setting, specifically within the 'Stay and Play' sessions she was responsible for leading. Nicky has carefully considered the approach she needed to take for her research to formulate a research design that fitted the scope of the project and her resources. This is explored more fully in Chapter 5.

Harriet

At the time of writing her study, Harriet was a third-year student doing a BA (Hons) in Early Childhood Professional Practice. She had taken advantage of some undergraduate research funding to work in Thailand and India and wanted to build on this experience in her research. She undertook her study to learn about how children from various cultural and ethnic backgrounds learn to develop in a social context in the educational setting within the UK. She wanted to find out how the 'home corner' within a nursery setting can provide positive interaction between children which maximises social development for children from diverse ethnic groups. Like Emily, she has had to consider her ethical approach to the sensitive subject and this is examined in Chapter 6.

Catherine

Originally a children's nurse, Catherine decided to pursue a teaching career and began her training in 2011, having completed a BA Integrated Early Childhood Top-up degree. She felt that her study would allow her an ideal opportunity to conduct research into the field of education in hospital. It was her hope that the evidence gathered as a result of her research might help to contribute to the improvement of early years education for children during their time in hospital and give a little back to the hospital that she admired very much. The research set out to identify how the education, social and emotional needs of children in their early years are met while in hospital, and looked at the challenges of providing play within the context of the Early Years Foundation Stage (EYFS) (DCSF, 2008) for children who are sick and experiencing often invasive treatment and who may have limited autonomy. Her analysis of data is discussed more fully in Chapter 7 as she brings her own perspective in attempting to understand a subject of real concern to her.

Before moving on to the opening chapter, we would like to take the opportunity to thank the students who have so freely given their studies for this book in order to help future students to have confidence in their approach to work based inquiry: as Nikki commented when reading the draft of the chapters drawing on her work: 'I wish I had this book when I started doing my research!'

1 Considering your research question

Choosing an appropriate research question can be the make or break of your study. In this chapter we encourage you to consider whether your question is:

- Purposeful, with potential for a positive impact upon your own practice and, ultimately, the experience of children and families;
- In an area that really interests you;
- Ethical and morally appropriate;
- Focused – will you be able to collect data to support it?
- A question that can actually be answered.

But we also acknowledge that we do not always get all of these things right first time, and that sometimes, some way into a project, your question might need to change.

This chapter is linked to Chapter 2, as we need to not only consider what makes a suitable research question, but also why we are driven to explore that particular area. Chapter 2 looks at our motivations for choosing the topic of study and the knowledge that we are bringing to it. In this chapter we focus upon choosing a suitable research question. Does the area of research that you are considering engage and motivate you? Is there real purpose to the question that you are asking? Is the question answerable and will its answer in some way have a positive impact upon the child and their family?

A number of research texts actually overlook the formulation of the research question and go straight to approaches. It is taken as a given that you know exactly what it is that you are looking for. In reality finding a suitable question is an extremely problematic stage during research design. The formulation of an appropriate question is vital, and unfortunately this is something that can often be done hastily. The result of this can be that when the student begins to collect (or worse still, to analyse) the data, they realise that they are unable to actually answer their original research question. In this chapter we look at a number of ways of avoiding this outcome.

Choosing a research question is inextricably linked to your choice of research approach, which will be discussed in Chapter 5. If you believe that there are definite answers out there to be found, then you will take a positivist approach to your research question. An example of this would be: 'What is the best way to teach counting in the early years?'. This suggests that there is one best way of teaching counting to be found and that numbers (or test results) can prove that. Of course, such a question precludes individual preferences and the huge range of contextual factors that can influence any given situation. As early years practitioners we tend, in general, to take a more non-positivist approach. Such an approach does not assume that there is one 'answer' which fits all situations, but that there is a whole range of views and opinions. This does not mean that we should not ask such questions, but that we should ask a question in a way that allows for variance and flexibility. So, in order to change the positivist question above to a non-positivist approach, a researcher might ask: 'What are some effective approaches to teaching counting in the early years?'. This approach allows a range of different possibilities and viewpoints to be explored.

At the heart of our question should be a desire to change things through expanding and deepening our knowledge and understanding. In McNiff's (2010) approach to action research she takes this one step further and specifies that the change should not be in 'things', but in us. Our desire should be to improve our own practice. The non-positivist type of question above has a number of benefits: the first is that it allows for variation in views and experiences within responses; and the second is it provides opportunity to value the views of the range of colleagues that the researcher might be working with. Reverend Astley (2011) highlighted the importance of us, as researchers, really *listening*. By sincerely doing this, as you seek to understand the other, it validates and honours their perspective. He adds that you give the gift of not only being heard but understood. By asking for the thoughts and feelings of others we are demanding a great deal, so we should remain aware of the responsibility that we have to value these.

Rather than seek a narrow answer, early years researchers will often collate a range of ideas and approaches from their research participants and use careful consideration of these to develop their own understanding and their own *practice*. In this way they use the data that they collect to construct a fuller understanding, this approach is known as a *constructivist* approach.

There is a range of questions to consider when deciding on the focus for your research, these include:

- Is it **ethical**? Or is there any possibility of it invading privacy or causing offence?

- Is it **purposeful** in that it will improve your understanding or your practice?

- Is it **specific and focused** enough for a small-scale project?

- Can the question that you have formulated **actually be answered**?

Although these may appear to be quite obvious elements, it is extremely rare for an initial question to effectively encompass them all. This is where the importance of discussing your question comes in. It is useful to discuss your question with peers; it is important that you discuss it with your tutor; but it is vital that you discuss it with your colleagues within the setting. Only by doing this can you be sure of the ethicality and purposefulness of your research.

It is normal for your research question to change as you develop a greater understanding of the area that you are looking into, but it is essential to establish a workable research question up front, so that you have 'a firm starting point for your research journey' (McNiff, 2010: 79). So, although you never know what obstacles you may face upon the way, or how your course may change, you need a clear view of the direction in which you are heading. Considering the points above will help with this. We will consider each of the areas in turn.

Ethicality

The ethical issue may appear to be quite a straightforward one, but students can often be unaware that their question could cause offence to someone or could be deemed obtrusive. For example, many students are very interested in parenting approaches. Dealing with problem behaviour, the frequency with which parents read with children and how much the child is allowed to use electronic games at home are the types of areas that students have brought to me as potential research areas in the past. Although there is no denying that these are really fascinating topics, there are two problems. The first, as Flick (2011: 23) points out, is that 'Answering the research question should lead to some sort of progress' which I am not convinced would be the case with the above topics. The second is that they are an ethical quagmire in terms of making judgements about parenting skills. When Roberts-Holmes (2011: 28) asks the question 'What do I want to change by doing my research?' the focus should always be upon our own, or our setting's, improvement; we should not have changing the practices of others as our main priority. This is neither ethical nor achievable. As early years practitioners, our focus should be on our practice within the setting, and interaction with parents within the setting can be a facet of that, but it is not appropriate for us to delve into what happens in the private, family home.

When considering a question, you should ask yourself 'What will it be helpful to find out more about, whose views would it be useful to hear, and how could this knowledge have a positive impact upon practices within their setting?'. So instead of 'How often does the average parent listen to their child read and how is that related to the child's progress in reading?', we could ask: 'How can our setting positively promote sharing story books as a fun and bonding activity for parents and children?'. The focus changes from what parents do, to what we can do to support children and their families.

In the earlier examples there is also the problem of the researcher appearing to 'judge' what others do. This is another ethical trap which should be avoided within your research. Finding out from people is very different to making judgements about people. The whole concept of practitioner research is for us to learn more about the practice in which we are developing our professionalism. Research should not be used as an excuse to stand in judgement of others, but to find out as much as possible about their reasons, motivations and restrictions, and by doing so attempt to find ways to negotiate these issues within our own practice. Seeking the views of colleagues in your setting on your research area will hopefully prevent this pitfall. MacNaughton et al. (2001: 3) state that:

> The best research will always involve close, ongoing collaboration between those who plan the research, those who carry it out, those who participate in it and those for whom the results have an impact.

Respect for those involved in your research is paramount. There is a strong intrinsic motivation when first embarking on research to want to find out if something is being done 'properly'. But does anyone really have the final say on what 'properly' is? One person's view on using the outdoors 'properly' is very different to the next person's. It is for this reason that terms such as 'How well is...?' or 'How effectively are...?' should be avoided, as we are really not in a position to answer such queries with any validity. Silverman (2000: 198) presents a beautifully tongue-in-cheek picture of this approach, whereby 'Under the remit of divine orthodoxy, the social scientist is transformed into philosopher-king (or queen) who can always see through people's claims and know better than they do'. This approach should be avoided at all costs. What is far more appropriate is to collate the views of others on areas that we are interested in and to explore these views, as it is likely that colleagues with greater experience in such situations will have a very different perception of the circumstances to you. It is important that you gain as much as possible from the extensive knowledge of *practice* that your colleagues in settings have, and reflect on this in relation to the *theory* that you have acquired.

The type of questions that students decide to research will often be along the lines of '*How well* is cultural diversity celebrated in nursery?'. In order to eliminate the implication of judgement on the part of the researcher it is useful to add that this is from a certain perspective, practitioners or parents for example. Or if the plan is to gather empirical evidence then something like 'How can cultural diversity be celebrated in nursery?' would take the stance of a more appreciative inquiry, looking for examples of good practice rather than assessing effectiveness. This would be ideal to carry out in collaboration *with*, as opposed to *on* your setting. Finally, a question like 'What approaches are taken to celebrating cultural diversity in nursery ... and what barriers still exist' indicates that the researcher is looking for positive examples but is aware that there are still areas for improvement. This provides a challenge for the researcher to use their evidence to consider the ways in which these barriers could be overcome.

> Ethicality has far more to it than just permission letters, as you will find in Chapter 3. It is all about the stance that we take when we carry out our research – and that starts with the formulation of the research question. It is important that we approach a study with humility and with the desire to learn from the experience, skills, knowledge and understanding of others. How will you make sure that your research question reflects such an approach?

rationale

Purpose

All of the studies that we look at in the course of this book have a very clear purpose in terms of the writers' own development. They sit very well within Roberts-Holmes' (2011: 29) advice to 'Be selfish' and 'Choose a topic which will be of benefit to your career'. They are both meaningful and worthwhile. Unfortunately some areas, as I've already mentioned, although very interesting, do not have such potential for impacting upon practice. One example that students are often attracted to, is healthy eating. This is another area where there is a tendency to make judgements about parenting skills, as it all too often falls into the 'monitoring what is in children's lunch boxes' approach. It is really important to remember that the focus of any study should be to provide us with an opportunity to improve our own practice and consider how we can improve the experience for children in our care. MacNaughton et al. (2001: 15) suggest that by ensuring that we undertake meaningful research 'it has some chance of making a difference to how we understand and practice our work with young children'. Monitoring the number of parents who provide unhealthy lunchboxes is not a way to do this.

What I can learn by asking & observing

Of course this topic, like most, could be made purposeful with the right approach. An important aspect of this process is to see 'what others have said and done in your area' (Roberts-Holmes, 2011: 31) through reading. As Roberts-Holmes (2011) points out, your focus could very well alter on consideration of existing viewpoints and discussion with others. As a result of her studies one student reasoned that her day-care nursery was providing their children with the vast majority of their nutrition for the day, and because of this she wanted to research healthy eating in order to provide the children with the best diet possible. This time there was no judgement of parents involved, just a desire to improve practice within the setting for the best outcomes of the child. She made the topic of healthy eating purposeful to her practice.

Already I hope you are beginning to see what is needed to make a research question as clear, focused and 'answerable' as it can possibly be. Cohen et al. (2007: 81) refer to this as *operationalisation*, whereby a general idea is translated into a 'specific, concrete question to which specific, concrete answers can be given'. Flick (2011) suggests that in order to test the appropriateness of a research question one should consider what possible answers to it might look like. If the question can be answered with 'very' or 'not very' then it probably needs slight rewording. Openings such as 'In what ways …?' or 'What are some of the approaches to/benefits of …?' give far greater scope for exploration and are far more meaningful.

Specificity and focus

Another difficulty when developing a research question is making sure that you are able to answer the question within the limitations of a very small-scale study. For example, many students are interested in the topic of using the outdoor area within early years. This often results in questions along the lines of: 'What benefits are there to using the outdoor area within the early years?'. Of course this is a vast topic and would result in a very superficial study if the student attempted to answer the question as it stands. MacNaughton et al. (2001) suggest that after thinking of a broad topic you should then divide it into sub-areas. Within those sub-areas there will be those factors that interest you more than others and those that are more meaningful than others. By doing this, less suitable areas can then be eliminated and an area can be chosen to look at in depth. Some examples of more specific questions that could be asked within the topic of outdoor play include:

- What are parents' perceptions of the benefits of outdoor learning activities?

- How can the outdoor area be used to support language development/numeracy skills?

- What are some of the ways that the outdoor area can support the development of social skills?

- What are children's perceptions of learning activities outdoors?

All of these questions could be specific and purposeful, but only if they are suitable for the context in which they are taking place. It could be that you have noticed that parents at a setting have misconceptions of the value of learning activities outdoors, meaning that they are reluctant for their children to participate. Without discovering what the perceptions of the parents actually are, the setting would not be able to provide them with the necessary information to tackle those misconceptions. It may be that you have noticed that children who are struggling with their communication (or numeracy) skills become less inhibited when involved in activities outdoors. How could this sense of freedom be used to maximise their development? And so on. I hope you see that by making the question more specific it can more directly relate to the needs of individual settings and their children and families. Mukherji and Albon (2010) urge students to discuss their areas of research interest with colleagues within the setting to see if they are able to pinpoint a specific area that needs further development. The more valuable and purposeful the research is to the setting, the more support you will gain in carrying it out.

One of the many reasons that the studies chosen for use in this book were successful was because there was a very specific focus and purpose to them. Harriet, for example, asks: 'How important is home corner role play to support children's social development in a culturally diverse context?'

She writes:

> The intention of this project is to investigate how the 'home corner' of an early childhood setting, used for the purposes of role-play, impacts on the social development of young children. This research, presented as a case study, focuses on the 'home corner' of one predominantly multicultural early years setting in a mixed nursery and reception class of an inner city primary school. As a result of consultation with the lead practitioner of the early years setting, it became apparent that the children aged two to five years originate from various parts of the world; namely Asia, Europe and the UK and speak a combination of languages; often with English as a new or additional language. This age phase has been selected for the research sample because as Rogers and Evans (2008) indicate, the ability to engage in pretence with peers is prominent between the nursery and reception phase, also reflecting personal observation in previous experience within the field of early childhood.
>
> In mentioning the term 'role-play' throughout this study, I refer to Hughes' Typology of Play (1996, cited in Lindon, 2001: 43) with a definition of role-play as: 'ways of exploring daily activities and actions,' alongside Featherstone and Cummings (2004) reference to role-play involving imitation and adopting the 'role' of another. By using the phrase 'home corner,' I propose
>
> Continues

Continued

the area dedicated to role-play in the focus setting which is resourced as a miniature domestic 'home' scene for children to play a multitude of predominantly 'family' roles. The research question also implies 'social development' as a central element of the study and for the purposes of this project, this is intended to suggest an array of social features that children acquire and use in their role-play. The EYFS (DCSF, 2008: 24) outlines one of six areas of learning and development as 'personal, social and emotional development,' referring to children in the social sense as acquiring: 'a positive sense of themselves and others; respect for others' and 'social skills,' of which a combination will be explored.

The certain emphasis of the research question on role-play and social development as well as the chosen setting to carry out the study is motivated by personal, professional, and current political issues. I have observed a variety of richly resourced role-play areas on practice in early childhood settings where children have generally appeared very enthused and engaged in such activity. With this in mind, I have always contemplated the impact that role-play has on the developing child, thus, this has stimulated my choice of research.

A further reason for focusing on children's social development for this study is due to its crucial place within children's school integration. For example, Marion (2000: 20) informs that typically a child in their first year of school is at a level where they are equipped to cope with: 'several peer relationships' and if at this age children are unable to connect with others, children may grow despondent. In this respect, social aspects of children's development appear of paramount importance to their emotional wellbeing which is of vital concern to a practitioner of the early years with children's welfare at the heart of their professional values. The importance of early social development also has a major impact on developing into future adults. This is supported by Marion (2000: 18) who argues that: 'The whole basis for young children and adults living and working together is founded on good relationships. This is clearly necessary for any successful community.' This statement advocates that positive association between individuals which ultimately requires a suitable level of social skill is a requirement for the presence of a cohesive society in which people can work alongside each other effectively.

Many students are interested in investigating role play, but Harriet included three specific criteria within her research question in order to narrow her focus. First, she specified the type of role play that she was interested in, showing her awareness that there are many different types. Secondly, she specified a certain area of development, social, rather than trying, as many students do, to look at the whole range of development. Finally, she specified the particular context (where the research is being carried out) as one which was culturally diverse. Not only does this enable Harriet to be far more concentrated when considering the type of data that she will collect, but it also narrows down the scope of her literature review. This, as you will discover in Chapter 6, will be a huge help to her.

Although there is no necessity to list the 'aims and objectives' of a project explicitly, it is useful to clarify them implicitly, as Harriet has done. While clarifying her objectives she also clarifies her research terms, for example what she means by the 'home corner', aware that the same term can hold different meanings for different people; MacNaughton et al. (2001) state that this type of explanation is vital to any research project. Under the umbrella of role play she teases out her main areas of interest: the displacement of children entering settings from different cultures and how role play can be used to help their integration into the social customs of their new culture, as well as providing an enjoyable vehicle for them to develop their social skills and relationships with peers.

I need to do this

Similarly, although Emily's research study, 'A snapshot of change and policy development in one children's centre: issues for consideration', was in danger of becoming wide and unmanageable due to change and policy development being sizeable areas for discussion, she skilfully narrows down the scope by stressing that she is only observing one children's centre and for a limited range of time (in this case seven months). The concept of taking a 'snapshot' of a development, by sitting it within a limited time frame, is a useful one. By using this approach Emily is able to focus on the events of a limited period of time in depth, rather than feeling that she needs to include every eventuality within the discussion. We shall discuss Emily's approach to her research further in the next chapter.

 When you decide on an area that interests you, think of its many components. For example, if you were interested in the topic of play, you might be interested in: definitions of play, parent and practitioner perceptions of play, imaginative play, role play, adult-initiated play activities, social development through play, risky play … the list is endless. When you think that you can begin to narrow it down to one area, then begin your reading and discuss your ideas with your peers and colleagues. By reading what authors have to say about the topic and by discussing it with others, specific points of importance and areas suitable for further investigation will begin to crystallise.

Can it be answered?

Roberts-Holmes (2011) suggests that you should 'think passionately with your heart and strategically with your head' when designing your research. Make sure that it is something that excites you, but make it manageable. I have lost count of the number of times that I have had to point out to students that their question cannot actually be answered. Some examples are below; see if you can work out what makes the questions impossible to answer with any validity:

- How important is superhero role play in boys' development?

- What influence does a daily exercise programme have on children's ability to learn?

- Which is more beneficial for children's development – free-flow play or structured activities?

There is a link between all of these questions, and that is the concept of development. How easy is it to measure a child's 'development' within a short period of time? This is a somewhat ethereal concept comprising numerous factors encompassing the child's physical, social, emotional and conceptual development. Speech, cognition, emotional awareness and dexterity are all a part of this. All of these questions imply that the researcher will be able to somehow measure the impact of their particular area of interest upon the child's development. Of course, this is impossible due to the numerous variables which impact upon a child from day to day. It may help to specify the area of development that you are focusing upon. But then consider this, if, for example, you chose to focus upon the social development aspect of boys' superhero role play, would the role play be the only interaction influencing the child during a 'typical' day? There are so many other interactions that the child en-counters, with parents, practitioners and peers, it would be foolhardy to suggest that just one aspect of that were influencing the child's develop-ment. The other problematic aspect that all of these questions embed is that they all involve numerous variables. It is difficult for scientists within laboratory conditions to 'prove' cause and effect, because there are always anomalies, it is all but impossible for a student to do so within a setting. All of these questions could be reworded to produce something that is closer to being answerable, here is an example:

- In what ways can superhero role play aid boys' social development?

Rewording this question has done two things: it has removed the notion of measurement (how important) and opened up the scope for seeking out positive examples. The researcher would still need to clarify that they were not attempting to present *all* of the ways that superhero role play might benefit boys, just those that they had observed or been made aware of through discussions. Another important action that the reword-ing has done is to narrow the area of development down to the 'social'. This means that the researcher can be far more specific in their literature review, observations and data-gathering. As it happens I still discouraged one student from pursuing this area of interest because of the very simple reason that it would be extremely difficult to collect any empirical data (you will find out more about types of data in Chapter 6). Although she could have reviewed literature and asked for the opinions of colleagues, she was not guaranteed to collate any further (observational) data without manufacturing a situation. What if the child/ren chose not to partake in superhero role play during her two weeks of observation? Would she tell them to do it? And then would that still be role play? This was a case where the question was actually a little too specific, and asking something more open-ended, such as 'What types of role play do boys engage in and how could these be used to support their social development?', may have been more beneficial. Can you see any way of making the other two questions more answerable?

Flick (2011: 24) states that 'research questions define not only what to study and how, but also which aspects of an issue remain excluded'. If it is not specifically mentioned within your question, then there is no necessity for you to cover it. Do not be tempted to take the 'kitchen sink' approach to research where you want to record everything of interest. Keep focused on your specific question and you will be able to explore it in depth, asking 'how' and 'why' questions rather than superficially presenting a breadth of information.

Can I change my question?

As I mentioned at the beginning of this chapter, at the outset of any journey it is helpful to have a fixed destination (McNiff, 2010), especially if your time is limited. Consulting literature and asking others' advice, particularly that of your colleagues, will help you to pinpoint the direction that you would like your research to take. Starting your research with a clear question will help you to achieve your goal within the set time. It will not eliminate all obstacles in your path, and it may have to be changed slightly, but it will give you a firm starting point.

MacNaughton et al. (2001: 9) comment that we need to be aware 'that sometimes the question that we start off with isn't the question that we end up researching, and that's okay'. Leanne certainly found this to be the case. She discovered that her focus of interest gradually altered during the course of her study. In her abstract she says:

This independent study tells the story of an investigation that I carried out in my setting related to child initiated learning. I discuss why I believe child initiated learning is important in a reception class. I focus on the views of practitioners and children

Continues

Continued

in the setting and compare these with current policy and relevant literature.

Research question

How can I improve my knowledge of child initiated learning and feel more confident facilitating it in a reception class?

When carrying out this study I originally had two aims:

- To improve my own knowledge and understanding of child initiated learning
- To develop more confidence to facilitate it in the classroom by listening to the views of colleagues, children and relevant literature.

As the study developed my focus changed to:

- How can staff ensure that they provide time for observations to be carried out on a regular basis in order to inform planning and 'tune into' children's interests?
- Can early years practitioners initiate change and improve outcomes for children through a work based inquiry?

It is not until near the end of the study that we find out why Leanne changed the focus of her study, but it is clear through her final bullet point that the process of carrying out a piece of research has been instrumental in transforming her views. At points throughout her study Leanne has included reflections on the sections that have gone before. After analysing her data she reflects on what she has learned through that process. She says:

Reflection part 2

This section of my inquiry reflects on the process by explaining what I learnt both personally and professionally about my issue after gaining insight from other practitioners and children. Swozdiak-Myers (2007) informs us that reflections are influenced by individual philosophy and personal beliefs. These principles are what prompted me to investigate this issue at the beginning. The study has enabled me to create a story based on real life ongoing practice. This has been enhanced because others have been able to participate in my study.

This inquiry has improved my understanding by making me aware that there are three types of child initiated activity and that self directed learning is associated with children showing interest, having ownership, choice and engagement in activities to enhance their learning and development. Looking at it from the lens of my colleagues has highlighted that we need to have a meeting to discuss and make all practitioners aware of the different forms of child initiated learning.

Space and time for interesting and fun activities should be provided in order to facilitate self directed learning. Carrying out regular observations provides vital opportunities to observe children's interests and cater for their individual needs. Appleby and Andrews (2012) say that reflective thinking leads to reflective learning. By reflecting on this issue, reading the literature and looking at it from my colleagues' lens I have discovered that we do not observe enough. Other practitioners share the same view. As a team we need to decide what reflective action needs to take place in order to make improvements.

I have learnt that the balance of child initiated activities depends on the practitioners' pedagogical approach which changes depending on the context, child and staff. Therefore when I am in my role as a teacher I will need to use my own judgement and knowledge of each child to assess the children's individual needs from observations. This will give me more confidence in deciding what the appropriate balance should be. Discussions with colleagues enabled me to learn from their advice and experience. My study kept evolving, McNiff and Whitehead (2009) point out that my research question and thinking will be refined as my analysis deepens due to reading, reflection and discussion. After evaluating my issue from different lenses the focus has changed to:

How can staff ensure that they provide time for observations to be carried out on a regular basis?

This demonstrates that my story is ongoing. This research inquiry has generated more questions that can lead to more investigations being carried out to further improve aspects of practice.

We often fail to make clear to students that with research you are venturing into the unknown; as McNiff (2011) has stressed, we are not travelling toward a set end-point, but stepping off a cliff and seeing what happens. And this is what should make it exciting, because each and every piece of research is unique; there are no right or wrong answers. Moustakas (1994: 65) comments that 'No scientific discovery is ever complete' and adds that 'The beauty of knowledge and discovery is that it keeps us forever awake, alive, and connected with what is and with what matters in life'. Leanne certainly demonstrates this connectedness in her research.

Key points from the chapter

It is likely that your time dedicated to your research project will expire long before your research journey seems 'complete'; as any good research should leave you brimming with new questions. But I cannot reiterate enough that time dedicated to an achievable research question before you set off on your journey will be time well spent. Have a look at the questions below, which comprise the titles of the studies explored in this text. Consider how far your thinking has moved on during the course of your engagement with this chapter, and see if you could have improved upon any of these questions.

- How well are children's needs met in hospital? (Catherine)
- How important is home corner role play to support children's social development in a culturally diverse context? (Harriet)
- Understanding the development of literacy skills within the early years – the creation of a supporting setting/parent partnership documentation. (Samantha)
- A snapshot of change and policy development in one children's centre: issues for consideration. (Emily)
- An investigation into working in partnership with parents and involving them in shaping services within a Sure Start children's centre. (Nikki)
- How can I improve my knowledge of child initiated learning and feel more confident facilitating it in a reception class? (Leanne)

Further reading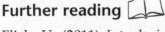

Flick, U. (2011) *Introducing Research Methodology. A Beginner's Guide to Doing a Research Project.* London: Sage.
Flick discusses how looking forward to the types of data that we might collect can help us to consider the appropriateness of our research question.
McNiff, J. and Whitehead, J. (2011) *All You Need to Know about Action Research.* 2nd edn. London: Sage.
McNiff and Whitehead encourage us to see our questions as open ended and as a means of discovering future areas of research.
MacNaughton, G., Rolfe, S.A. and Siraj-Blatchford, I. (2001) *Doing Early Childhood Research.* Buckingham: Open University Press.
MacNaughton et al. encourage us to consider the impact that our research might have upon the settings within which we are working.

2 Theoretical framework

In this chapter we will explore how:

- It is important to be clear about the beliefs and experiences with which you are approaching your study;
- No one can approach a study as a completely objective observer – it is important that you explain where your interest has emerged from;
- You must be clear about your current views, how those were created, and what you are you hoping to discover through your study.

A number of my colleagues are not great fans of the term 'theoretical framework' as they feel that it is too easily confused with the literature review, but it is because of its close affinity to reviewing literature that I think that we should use it. We are happy to talk about the 'theory' of academics that have authored book chapters and journal articles, but we are not so happy using the term in relation to our own ideas. The fact is that our own ideas are equally important, we are entitled to our own 'theory', and it is this theory that provides the framework for any study that we carry out. It is for this reason that I believe that the term 'theoretical framework' fits perfectly, but other terms such as 'personal research stories' (Roberts-Holmes, 2011) can also be used. It is up to you to decide which phraseology is most akin to your own understanding and approach.

It is important within your study to explain not only the ideas and beliefs that frame your work, but also where these have emerged from. What life experiences, significant reading and professional encounters have formed the basis of your beliefs? It may be that one incident in practice or one particular text significantly changed your outlook on the topic that you are exploring. A number of research textbooks completely overlook this aspect of the research approach, but I believe that it is vitally important that you share these details and explain why they have had such an effect. Ely (1999: 122) explains why extremely effectively:

> The investigator wants to understand the minds and the hearts of the research participants in as total and unadulterated a way as possible. To do so s/he must attempt to recognize personal prejudices, stereo-types, myths, assumptions, and other thoughts and feelings that may cloud or distort the perception of other people's experiences. I do not believe that we lose subjectivity, for human perception is by nature and definition subjective. I do believe that by acknowledging our own myths and prejudices, we can more effectively put them in their place. I also believe that greater self-knowledge can help us to separate out thoughts and feelings from those of our research participants, to be less judgemental, and to appreciate experiences that deviate greatly from our own.

Although the traditional and persisting view of research is that of the detached observer, as Ely points out, it is impossible to eliminate all subjectivity from a study, so instead we need to be transparent about our motivations. By doing this we increase, rather than lose, the rigour of our work. Roberts-Holmes (2011: 23) stresses that our 'personal motivations are part of generating the methodology, validity and authenticity of the research project' (ibid.: 27). He adds that sometimes our research is as much about discovering ourselves and our life influences as it is about learning from others.

The theoretical framework, to some extent, replaces and surpasses the traditional 'hypothesis' as discussed by Bell (1993). The hypothesis was embedded within the foundation of having certain presumptions, or hunches, which researchers then attempted to 'test' through the research in a pseudo-positivist way. It goes without saying that we have since moved on from the 'experimental' approach as educational research has more readily aligned itself with anti-positivism, or constructivism, but another flaw of this approach was that there was no requirement for the researcher to explain where that 'hunch' had developed from. Was it based upon life and professional experience and hence a valuable and relevant area for the researcher to explore, or was it simply plucked from the ether? With the hypothesis approach there is the risk of 'research for the sake of research' rather than a purposeful approach to discovery which will benefit the researcher, and so, ultimately, the child.

When Bell talked about deciding on a research topic in 1993, the fact that it 'may even have some practical application later on' (Bell, 1993: 16) was the *last* of her four reasons for choosing a topic. Such is not the case for us as *practitioners*, when the whole aim of our carrying out research is in order to improve our *practice*. It may be that we do not choose a small, neat project that fits perfectly into our time slot, but that we begin the first cycle of a project that may take years to complete. That you will be able to complete your study was the second of Bell's (1993) list of priorities, but I must agree with McNiff (2010) on this and ask whether research can ever be deemed 'complete'. She states 'There is no final answer to anything. Knowledge can be created as well as discovered' (McNiff, 2010: 28). As I mentioned in the last chapter the best research raises the greatest number of questions which require further investigation.

Roberts-Holmes (2011) repeatedly refers to the 'motivation' behind a project. What drives the researcher to pursue that area of research? Establishing the relevance of the study to the researcher is vital if a meaningful piece of work is to be produced. And this is exactly what Emily does. In this excerpt Emily uses her theoretical framework to clearly explain why she chose to explore the impact of policy development on one children's centre, and how she hoped that the findings would benefit both herself and her colleagues. She writes:

This study will provide a snapshot of one Sure Start children's centre (SSCC) during a period of change and policy development. It is perhaps important to provide an introduction to the centre and why it was chosen for this case study, along with an explanation of my own professional role. I currently work as a family support worker in this large and newly developed SSCC which is based within a largely rural community. This children's centre has been developed during phase two of the previous Labour Government's policy of establishing a children's centre within each community across the country. Sure Start was established in 1997 with the intention of improving outcomes for children in disadvantaged areas and paved the way for the development of the SSCC in 2004. The remit of Sure Start was to bring together early years education, health and family support to improve the outcomes of children under the age of four living in disadvantaged areas (DCSF, 2009). Improving outcomes for children in this way very much reflected upon my own value base as an early years practitioner.

I have been working in the Early Years Sector for thirteen years, since the birth of my first child in 1997. My personal, professional and academic progress has developed in parallel to the development of Sure Start and the many changes in the early years sector over these past thirteen years. My personal experiences as a mother of three children and my professional experience as pre-school supervisor has [sic] provided the background and knowledge which has led to a career in family support. As my professional role has developed, supported by my academic development, I have gained a better understanding of the importance of multi-agency working in ensuring that the needs of families are met. The ethos of SSCCs was very much something which I desired to be part of professionally.

Continues

Continued

Therefore, setting out to research multi-agency working within children centre's was an emotive subject choice, based upon my own strong value base and professional history. However, as I began my study a huge earthquake of change began to affect not only the centre within which I was based but the very future of SSCCs across the United Kingdom. There are currently 3500 children's centres open in the United Kingdom. These now have a statutory legal basis and will be inspected by the Office for Standards in Education (OFSTED). However, the general election of May 2010 led to the historic instalment of a coalition government taking over from the Labour Party who had introduced and nurtured Sure Start, pouring an estimated 1.4 billion per year into the programme (Cassidy, 2009). The combination of the current unstable financial climate and an era of change and new policy under the new administration has [sic] left many supporters of Sure Start feeling insecure.

The future for Sure Start and even my own professional role under the new government remains unclear. Although the funding for Sure Start had been ring-fenced by the previous administration until 2010, there are no concrete guarantees that the funding and government backing will continue. Already we have seen the Sure Start maternity grant cut and local authorities have responded anxiously by freezing decisions regarding funding, recruitment and building work for any ongoing developments of children's centres. It could be considered that such unrest and anxiety will have an inevitable effect upon the staff, families and children who have embraced children centre's as part of their communities.

This study will present a snapshot of one children's centre during this turbulent period. My research has provided a picture of practice within the centre in order to identify if the process of change and policy development experienced at both a national and local level has had an impact upon professional practice. The evidence collected has been separated into three clear themes which will be discussed in more detail:

- Tensions – difficulties experienced due to changes and new policies
- Interprofessional working – staff members' perception of interprofessional working and co-location
- Meeting needs – identifying if and how the needs of disadvantaged children are being met

The information provided in this study as a result of my research is intended to inform and challenge views and allow for debate between colleagues. Although it could be ultimately argued that the purpose of this study is to graduate from the Early Years Foundation Degree, it is my sincere desire that I will be able to influence and inform those people who are in a position to secure the future of Sure Start Children's Centres within the community.

Commentary

With this framework Emily achieves a number of objectives. First, she effectively contextualises her study in terms of where the study is actually taking place, why it was chosen and her role within that context. As is explored with the issue of 'insider and outsider' research in Chapter 3, all early years practitioners undertaking research actually have dual roles; for the purposes of the study they become a researcher, but they also hold another role within the setting, or the arena in which the research is taking place. They may be a student voluntarily gaining experience, or they may be practitioner, manager, parent, childminder, teaching assistant and so on. Because of the impact that this other role will have on access and relationships within the research context, it is important that it is established at the very beginning of the research. Cohen et al. (2000: 140) investigate a number of theorists' views on naturalistic or ethnographic research, through which the researcher explores a social reality naturalistically and develops their own theory from the data they collect. What comes through very strongly in the majority of the interpretations is the visible presence of the researcher within the study, and that because of this there is a need for their 'personal, social and interactional position in the situation' to be fully explained. Emily succeeds in doing this in her first two paragraphs.

Secondly, Emily establishes her value base. She does not pretend indifference around the topic of multi-agency working; instead she states that due to her life and professional experience she views multi-agency working as vitally important. She opens herself up to scrutiny as an integral element in the process of the research (MacNaughton et al., 2001). The third thing that Emily does, and very well, is something that many students forget to include, she succinctly contextualises her study in terms of the current socio-political situation and the current policy context. This is something that should be an integral part of your literature review, and so will be revisited in Chapter 4, but it should also be touched upon at the start of your study in order to show the relevance of your topic within the present social climate. As Mukherji and Albon (2010: 188) point out, an interpretivist approach to research is about 'making sense of the researcher's immediate world', as such it is important to give as detailed a picture of that world as possible.

Emily states that the aims of this research are to provoke debate between her colleagues, but also to potentially influence those government bodies whose decisions impact upon practice and lives. This seems ambitious, but it should be an aim of all quality research. Why should Emily's voice not be heard over those of theorists who have little or no current practice experience? What actually happens to your research, how it is *disseminated* is discussed fully in Chapter 9. Pieces of research should be living, working documents, not just something to fulfil the requirements of a degree and then sit on a shelf.

Samantha clearly wanted her research to be a tool for impacting upon quality in her setting. In her theoretical framework she says:

I am a manager of an 'outstanding' setting and with a team of passionate early years practitioners promote literacy everywhere within the setting. We use a variety of activities inspired by children's interests and schemas, be it spontaneous or next step planning creatively devised by a team of skilled practitioners.

As part of our commitment to quality improvements every term we provide questionnaires for parents to feedback their views on the quality of the setting. I was dismayed when analysing the spring term questionnaires because under the question 'how do you rate the level of education provided in the setting?' we had a significant proportion graded at 'satisfactory' with additional comments requesting to see more development in reading and writing skills.

As a team we agreed that further investigation into this was a top priority and we wanted the opportunity to critically review our approach to developing literacy within the setting and identify if it was:

a) Lack of consistency within our planning,

b) Or a communication issue as parents do not understand how we as practitioners embed literacy skills on a day to day basis.

I also wanted the opportunity to extend and develop a better community of practice by opening up the research process to a panel of participants that included all staff, parent representatives, committee members and teachers. I am a true ambassador of community practice and believe 'getting it right' isn't down to just one person or one body of professionals.

Throughout my experience and research as a professional working in early years I have come to appreciate the complexity of literacy development and interestingly, within the Bercow review (DCSF, 2008) evidence illustrates that there is insufficient understanding of the centrality of speech, language and communication amongst professionals, policy makers and parents and families themselves. This raises the question of why supporting guidance and set curricula are inconsistent and unclear.

It is important to state at this point that during the research process of this paper, the nation's educational stance within early years was in a situation of pending change. Referring to the early year's curriculum, Teather (2011) explained why the government had requested a review of the Early Years Foundation Stage (EYFS) (DCSF, 2008). Her response was:

'The intention is to set out a much slimmer, easier to understand early year's curriculum. It will give professionals more freedom in how they work with children, and will involve parents more in their child's learning. Fundamentally, it will make sure we are preparing our children for the challenges of school and beyond. This isn't just about making sure they can hold a pencil, children need the resilience, confidence and personal skills to be able to learn'. (Roberts: Nursery World July 2011)

It clearly implies that the review will provide more effective guidance and as an experienced practitioner within the Early Years I am very aware of the need and benefits for change and evolution to keep up with the needs of society.

Therefore, even though my research is set against a background of uncertainty and unclear expectations of literacy from the government, this opportunity has still been beneficial to the development of the setting and the community of practice. I hope that this research will result in an insight that will be complementary to the revised EYFS when it is put into place.

Commentary

Cohen and Manion (1989: 223) describe action research as 'an on-the-spot procedure designed with a concrete problem located in an immediate situation' and this certainly appears to be Samantha's approach to her research. She has a problem and she would like to solve it. Samantha is extremely honest and open in sharing her disappointment at discovering an area of weakness that she was unaware of. Her genuine desire to get to the bottom of that problem and solve it gives a real drive and purpose to her research. McNiff (2010: 82) puts it this way:

Asking the question, 'Why am I concerned?' is important because in all approaches it is important to give a rationale for the research, and say why it should be done in the first place. Unless you do this, your research could be seen as simply a good idea, but without a solid reason or purpose.

By sharing her 'concerns' Samantha gives a clear justification, or a solid reasoning for this area of research. Roberts-Holmes (2011: 27) states that 'Your personal motivations are part of generating the methodology, validity and authenticity of the research project', and I am sure that you will agree that Samantha's frankness in acknowledging a shortfall within her setting encourages you as reader to accept the validity of what she is saying.

Samantha goes on, very effectively and succinctly, to share some of her key ideologies about early years practice. McNiff's (2010: 83) view is that 'The issue of values and how you are living out your values is central in action research'. In just one sentence Samantha establishes that she sees teamwork and collaboration as vital for effective practice. Because 'there are multiple interpretations of, and perspectives on, single events and situations' (Cohen et al., 2001: 22) it is important to be transparent about what lens you are using to look at the situation. And Samantha makes clear that hers are the views of someone who regards community values, rather than individualism very highly. For her, collaborative working is central to quality practice, and this will inevitably influence her interpretation of data. Costley et al. (2010: 33) comment that it is 'important to articulate your own perspectives or premises clearly' because 'This process of articulating your own position will allow others to reflect on alternative constructions'. As Samantha has made us aware of her viewpoint we can take this into account, and the authenticity of her work is not jeopardised.

 What are some of your key beliefs as a practitioner and how might these impact upon your own study? If you are unsure of your own ideology then imagine that you are establishing a nursery of your own. If you had to make a statement of the key beliefs and values of that nursery then what would the statement include? At this nursery we aim to … What do you see as most important to you in your role as an early years practitioner?

Samantha shows a good understanding that 'Social science … [is] a subjective rather than an objective undertaking' (Cohen et al., 2001: 20) and she makes clear to us her particular areas of interest, her strengths and her weaknesses. She also recognises that naturalistic research is 'a means of dealing with the direct experience of people in different contexts' (ibid.). By 'context' I do not only mean the setting itself, but the wider context that was discussed earlier with reference to Emily's study. This can be viewed in the same way that we view Bronfenbrenner's (1979) micro, meso and macro systems. There are the practices of the immediate setting in which the researcher is situated, but these are influenced by many external factors, from parents to local and national policy. Within your particular area of interest what are the current factors that are influencing thinking and practice? Samantha states that those issues that she is exploring are currently in a state of flux as the early years curriculum is being revised. Emily is very positive about these changes, a frame of mind that is sometimes difficult to maintain when there is continued uncertainty.

Below, Leanne gives a brief introduction to the context of her research, and then places herself at the very heart of her own study:

I have worked as a Teaching assistant in a school setting for fifteen years. I have experience working in the Foundation Stage and Key Stage One. I currently work in the reception class of a large primary school in an urban area. There are 460 children attending the school. The foundation unit has a nursery that provides morning and afternoon places for forty children. There are also two reception classes that each has [sic] thirty children. Twelve practitioners are employed in the early years department these include: three teachers, four teaching assistants and five learning support assistants.

Brookfield (1995) makes it clear that practitioners should examine issues from their own lens as an autobiography of their practice. I looked at this issue from my own perspective. Denscombe (2003) says that practitioners can benefit from action research because it is part of their professional self-development. I learnt how to improve aspects of my own professional practice and tried to influence other practitioners into changing or improving parts of their practice. Appleby and Andrews (2012) make it clear that as a practitioner I must recognise and understand my own values and beliefs because they influence my actions. McNiff et al. (2003) point out that practitioners examine issues that are important to them. This research is significant to me for both personal and professional reasons. Bolton (2010) says that by writing about this issue I demonstrate that I am eager to explore how my personal and professional self interrelates.

From my experience as an early years practitioner and mother of two boys I believe that children should be active learners who are able to make choices. They should have ownership of their ideas and experiences. The DCSF (2009) inform us that the activities children choose are the driving force for enhancing their knowledge and ability. I have had the privilege to witness this first hand. Children should be allowed the freedom to explore new areas and discover new

Continues

Continued

concepts alone and with their peers in order to enhance learning. As I have seen with the children in my setting and my own sons, children can learn a considerable amount when they are deeply absorbed in free choice activities. I also appreciate that structure and teacher led activities are required in order for practitioners to model activities or take the lead by talking about a specific feature of learning or by discussing something in particular. Experience in my setting has made me aware that it would be chaotic if children did not have direction from adults and always chose their own activities.

My ultimate goal is to become an early years teacher. During my training and experience working with different practitioners I became confused as to what child initiated learning actually was and unsure how much time should be allocated to this in the foundation stage. In my future role I want to be more knowledgeable about the value of this style of learning and demonstrate more confidence in providing opportunities to cater for children's individual interests. McNiff et al. (2003) acknowledge that by carrying out action research staff can improve their own understanding of issues. Swozdiak-Myers (2007) also points out that action research can be linked with reflective practice because both are ongoing processes where practitioners increase their knowledge which enables them to alter or enhance future practice. Through my inquiry I have reflected on what I have learnt about myself and my subject. I have also been able to increase my awareness of how children learn through self-directed activity.

Commentary

Leanne's is very much a post-structuralist approach to research. Within post-structuralism it is not only the research subjects that are under the microscope (so to speak) but 'the research project itself, especially the lenses and the actions of the researcher' (MacNaughton et al., 2001: 58). Rather than feign a detached objectivity, it is fine to say 'here I am, I am part of this work'. Leanne also relates the research to her personal life, and it is usual that the things that interest us most within practice will have a very personal significance. These topics may be related to our own childhood, our knowledge of the children and families that we have worked with over the years or the experience of our own children. Becoming a parent yourself can have a significant effect on your thinking. As a primary school teacher I always had the same expectations of both boys and girls, and I realise now that this was not always helpful. Having now brought up two very lively boys of my own, I am aware that some boys benefit from a far more active approach; they can find sitting and listening for periods of time far more difficult than girls. I did not know this until experiencing it for myself as a

What experience has created your interest?

- Your own personal life experience
- Your professional experience

Where has your current knowledge/ views of the area come from?

- Do you have knowledge of this area within theory or policy?
- Have you sought others' views around this area?

Within which context will you be exploring it?

- What will your role be in carrying out this research?
- Where will the research be taking place?

Figure 2.1 Your professional journey towards establishing a theoretical framework

parent. Leanne has learnt a lot from observing her own children, and it is good to take the knowledge that we develop as parents into practice.

Glesne and Peshkin (1992: 104) stress that carrying these experiences into your research is not a fault, it is a quality; they say 'My subjectivity is the basis for the story that I am able to tell. It is a strength on which I build. It makes me who I am as a person and a researcher'. I like Glesne and Peshkin's comparison of presenting research to telling a story because that is what you are doing. Most importantly you are telling the story of what you have learnt and you cannot show the end point in that process without making clear where, exactly, you began. Leanne does this by saying 'I had a good idea about the benefits of free choice activities for children through my personal and professional experience and through my familiarity with policy, but what I wasn't so sure of was this ...'. When we read Leanne's study we are not reading solely about facts that have been discovered, we are reading the story of Leanne's transformation in thinking.

If you are considering an area of study while you are reading this then stop and contemplate why it is that area appeals to you. What is your experience of it? Is it something that you consider to be problematic or positive? Where have your views come from, life experience, work experience, literature, or a combination? What are you hoping to achieve by researching into this area? The more transparent you can be about these factors at the outset of your study, the more validity and credibility you will give your work.

Key points from the chapter

Remember that within practitioner research 'Knower and known are interactive, inseparable' and that for this reason 'inquiries are influenced by the inquirer values' (Cohen et al., 2001: 137). Because of this we must be clear about our values and from where they have emerged. It is important to be transparent about the knowledge that we hold as we begin our research journey and what we actually hope to achieve with the research. Remember, self-improvement should be central to all practitioner research.

Further reading

Cohen, L., Manion, L. and Morrison, K. (2007) *Research Methods in Education*. 6th edn. London: RoutledgeFalmer.
Cohen et al. discuss the subjective nature of research in the social sciences.
Costley, C., Elliott, G. and Gibbs, P. (2010) *Doing Work-based Research: Approaches to Enquiry for Insider Researchers*. London: Sage.
This book is an excellent resource for students undertaking practitioner research and addresses the complexities and challenges of working as an insider to the setting both as an employee or student familiar with the setting.
Ely, M. (1991) *Doing Qualitative Research: Circles within Circles*. London: Falmer Press.
Ely discusses how the researcher is entwined within the research process.

3 Taking an ethical stance

Having a section on ethics within your study is a must if you want to ensure that your study passes, but a really good study will have ethics, or a sense of what is 'morally right', underpinning it throughout.

This chapter will consider:

- The delicate balance of responsibility between being a practitioner and a researcher within your setting;
- The insider/outsider position within your inquiry;
- Researcher bias;
- Informed consent and assent;
- Researching with children;
- Guidance that can help you to formulate your ethical stance and underpin your study.

Undertaking an ethical study is far more than simply a matter of gaining consent through a permission letter. It is not a tick-box exercise and your approach to this needs careful thought. For example, researching with children can be a potentially exciting and rich experience which can lead to invaluable insights but requires sensitivity and planning if you are to ensure that no harm comes to them through your actions. Your commitment to an ethical approach, which takes account of the role you play in relation to other practitioners and professionals, parents and children should be evidenced through your practice in building trusting relationships which allow for a partnership approach to your work. This approach inherently calls for a responsibility to responding to the potential unforeseen sensitivities which may arise throughout as a result of your inquiry. The steps in your thinking need to be recorded so that the reader can have a sense of the issues involved in your study and how you worked through them. Including your ethical audit trail, for example meetings with your supervisor, ethics proposal forms and sign-off sheets in your appendices is important in showing your commitment to taking an ethical approach. This adds to the reliability and credibility of your inquiry.

Let us start by looking at some strong examples of an ethicality section. Emily shows real sensitivity to the feelings of her participants in her study.

She writes:

> My study aimed to provide a snapshot during an uncertain time. As a Family Support worker based in the team my inquiry posed a question of ethical sensitivity. Some of the participants felt high levels of anxiety and emotional stress due to the uncertain future of Sure Start and changes in policy. Although it would have provided a very useful perspective, and may have enhanced my inquiry, it would have been inappropriate to explore these feelings and thoughts further without risking distress to the participants. This is supported by the British Educational Research Association (BERA, 2011) guidelines which remind us as researchers to do no harm. Although the participants in question felt strongly that their opinion must be noted regarding the effect of policy change, it was agreed that participation in the semi structured interview would perhaps not be the most appropriate method of recording this valuable information. Instead it was agreed to record conversations with a purpose, as they arose, which place no additional pressure on an already sensitive issue.
>
> The topic choice was a personal issue, and raised possible issues about researcher bias. Although I have my own value base about supporting families it was important to not introduce my own thoughts when carrying out my inquiry. This has not been easy, and perhaps reflects upon my dual role as children's centre employee and researcher. It was important to identify if the changes taking place had an impact upon the families accessing the centre. However, to raise this question to [sic] the parents themselves would presuppose the suggestion that there could be a negative impact, where in fact there may not be. Therefore, my earlier intention to send a questionnaire to parents was deemed to be unhelpful, and instead the opinions of staff members about this issue were sought.

Commentary

As you can see Emily was concerned that no one should be harmed by her actions and she has gone to great pains to think through how she might ensure the safety of her participants using well-established guidelines and theory to underpin her work. Through this we can see that she has taken a personal approach by researching *'with'* as opposed to *'on'* participants (James, 2004). She has explained her position as a member of the team in which she has set her enquiry and explored the delicate balance between being a researcher and also a practitioner. This is an area which needs to be considered within all work-based inquiry as you will need to acknowledge the extent to which you are part of the setting and the implications this has for your study. Emily, in this example, has worked through the issues involved in carrying out her inquiry. She demonstrates the moral principles and values underpinning her work and decides that getting as much data as possible does not justify jeopardising the well-being and safety of her colleagues. She acknowledges that her study may not have been as complete as she would have liked because she was aware of the profound implications of using any means to justify the outcomes gained. This implies a respect for her participants' feelings as adults caught in the midst of policy change within the children's centre and acknowledges that her need for insight and information into their thoughts and feelings about this did not justify causing distress and upset to them. Emily points to the need for her to bear this in mind when considering who to include in her study. She decided not to include parents although this would have given her a richer picture, as to do so would have raised anxieties that services would be potentially reduced. Consequently she changed her proposed methods of data collection from questionnaires and interviews to recording conversations with a purpose.

McNiff (2011) has made this approach clearer for us in highlighting the 'balcony' view of inquiry where the researcher acts as a spectator and the research arena sits outside the researcher. She argues the need to acknowledge that you are part of the world and a part of the study. It is worth exploring what that means for you in the context of your study and the implications in taking part in work-based inquiry as a part of a setting. For example, considering your position as to whether you are an insider or an outsider within the inquiry is an important aspect of your ethical stance. This relates to the issue of the potential power you have in respect of participants which must be understood and thought through before embarking on your study. As Floyd and Linet (2010: 5) write 'although a potential minefield, insider research can also be a rich pasture, from which important data can be harvested, with appropriate boundaries to satisfy ethical concerns'. Your presence will have an effect on the setting, and will impact on the unspoken issues. It will have an effect on the politics within the setting and your responsibility as a 'virtuous' researcher who shows trust, kindness, modesty and humility (Stern, 2011) is to make sure that the impact that you have is a positive one. It is important that you also consider these qualities as a basis for your approach to your written submission in terms of asserting your beliefs, commitments and interests. This will help to secure the validity and credibility of your research as it acts in triangulation with your theories and research practices (Formosinho and Formosinho, 2012). This is explored more fully in Chapter 6.

Reed and Walker (2012) explored the phenomenon of insider/outsider inquiry in their work with students. At the end of their 14-month inquiry into students forming a 'community of practice' to publish their work-based inquiry abstracts, they concluded that being insider or outsider is not, in itself, the real issue. What is important is recognising the shifts in balance that occur and asking whether this makes a difference to the results of the inquiry and whether it helps or inhibits inquiry practice. This is worth teasing out and debating within your study.

As Emily's work indicates, her workplace could be described as a 'community of practice' (Wenger, 1998, 2010; Wenger et al., 2002) which implies a mutual engagement between practitioners, joint enterprise with parents and children, and shared repertoires or ways of practising. Effectively, this means the setting doing things with others that have an agreed purpose, shared expectations and shared experience, and finding ways of developing strategies to solve problems. Communities have specific ways of functioning which you will either be privy to as a member of that community, or which you will be joining as an 'outsider'; and sometimes negotiating access will require personal qualities of humility, patience, empathy and respect (Costley et al., 2010). It will need skills of communication, negotiation and clarity of purpose. How you negotiate with the setting and position your study within it will have implications for how your inquiry progresses. It may well be worth considering how the project will benefit the setting. Will it be of value to them or are you simply utilising them in order to obtain your qualification or degree?

Once again, Emily demonstrates the level of trust she had within her community of practice and with this her responsibility not to use this to the detriment of her colleagues, parents and ultimately children. As Costley et al. (2010: 57) write: 'The application of care is not a sentimental approach to inquiry: it is about how researchers can best meet their caring responsibilities'. This may require consideration of the accepted practices of the setting to unpicking the underpinning issues and the different and sometimes conflicting needs of participants to develop your own position informed by literature and theory. As Rawlings (2008) points out, as well as understanding the requirements of ethical practice, how you feel about what you are doing plays an important part in your approach.

It may well be that you hold a position of authority within the organisation or that you work as a colleague and have built up trusting relationships where information is freely exchanged within the context of your setting and profession.

How will you continue to manage these relationships through-out the study and afterwards?

You may be entering a setting for the purpose of undertaking a study but you will still be joining and working as part of the team. As a researcher you are in a privileged position.

How will you acknowledge the impact that you will have?

Researcher bias

Emily goes on to consider the potential for researcher bias as she acknowledges her personal interest in the research topic and the complexities and difficulties in not imposing her own feelings and opinions onto the data. As she points out, this is complicated by her insider role as a practitioner and member of the team. She has been proactive in recognising this and in working through the issues that this has presented. The extent to which your inquiry raises personal issues for you is important to acknowledge both to yourself and to the reader as was explored fully in Chapter 2. This does not mean baring your soul but being honest about the motivation for your inquiry and the rationale for it. It is good advice to choose a research topic of interest to you and meaningful to both yourself and your setting. If the inquiry will not ultimately benefit the children in your setting in some way, then is it really worth exploring? Whatever your chosen area of inquiry, the interplay between your views, experiences and values and the way you go about your inquiry in relation to others requires clarity.

Harriet

Harriet also demonstrates a strong ethics section as she, like Emily, places the best interests of those she is researching with at the heart of her study and the preparation for it. For example, she considers the issues of consent in detail.

She writes:

Research ethics is concerned with 'a duty of care in relation to all those participating in the research process' (Burton et al., 2008: 50) as well as the moral judgements about the aims and methods of the inquiry (Aubrey et al., 2010). It is therefore possible to suggest that ethical considerations in a study reflect a respectful attitude towards the inquiry sample with their best interests as central to data collection. A significant element of this study to support ethical practice is the priority of informed consent which ensures 'trust' between the researcher and inquiry sample and gives research participants an opportunity to choose or discard participation having been provided with 'all the relevant information' about the project (Roberts-Holmes, 2005: 60). Anderson and Arsenault (1998: 19) identify that such relevant information will include clarity of the 'purpose of the research', the 'benefits' in becoming a participant, the agreement to address participants' queries regarding the process and the opportunity 'to withdraw' from the inquiry at any stage the participant chooses. In order to ensure that participants can give informed consent before research implementation, I have designed informed consent letters to receive the necessary permission from relevant participants. The letters include all of the required information to allow the sample to fully comprehend the research process.

The gatekeeper, in this instance, the manager of the early years setting will be provided with an informed consent letter so as initial permission for the research can be obtained with their full awareness of the nature of the research (Roberts-Holmes, 2005). By asking for the manager's 'signature' on the informed consent documents 'proof' is provided that they are willing to allow the research to be carried out in their setting and that they completely understand the procedure (Cannold, 2001: 184). For both the practitioner and parent interviews, informed consent letters will also be provided for participants outlining the process of the research and use of their data and a signature will also be required to demonstrate an agreement of participation.

For research methods directly involving children narrative observations and child conferencing, there is reason to speak to them about the methods and allow for their vocal response to participate (Roberts-Holmes, 2005). Consequently, I aim to provide simplified explanations to children about the research. However, this may be challenging to comprehend for very young children of diverse linguistic backgrounds. Consequently, all parents at the setting are to be provided with an informed consent letter regarding the principles. However, language is a barrier to understanding the letters for several parents who speak English as an additional language or have limited English vocabulary (Anderson and Arsenault, 1998). Subsequently, the co-operation of an Early Years Practitioner that is able to translate the content of the letter to parents will enable their informed choice for their child's participation (Coady, 2001). Furthermore, Anderson and Arsenault (1998: 20) describe confidentiality as the notion of how information expressed during research will be implemented in the project and that 'the identity of the individual will remain anonymous'. To ensure this ethical principle, as well as providing participants with an explanation of 'how the data they provide will be used' through informed consent letters (Anderson and Arsenault, 1998: 20), the documentation promises to remove the names of the setting, staff and children from the data collected to make certain participants' identities cannot be recognised in the research.

Informed consent

Harriet has discussed the need to consider informed consent as a priority and how essential it is to the building of trust between the researcher and participant. She outlines what she means by this, including the importance of providing clear and honest information about the study and what their participation involves, the understanding that they can withdraw at any point without repercussions and, importantly, the benefits of the inquiry to participants and the organisation. Harriet makes clear her undertakings to her participants which she details in her consent letter. This includes information concerning anonymity, confidentiality, recording, storage of data, how long the data will be kept after the inquiry has finished and who will read the finished work. These are all essential areas to cover. However, Harriet has looked at the issue more widely in considering her participants' needs as she gives examples of parents needing support with literacy and language and explains her plans for those of them not being able to give informed consent. Thought has been given to the language used, in that jargon will need to be explained and understanding cannot always be taken for granted. Harriet adhered to her code of ethics as an early years practitioner, which includes making sure she delivers what she promises or explains why not, being honest and open with participants and always putting their interests first, not making assumptions or judgements. She ensures that she works at their pace. In this way she engenders trust with her participants and removes any potential barriers to their participation.

Children at the forefront

You will notice that both examples place the child at the centre of their thoughts and plans and that consideration of their welfare and well-being are paramount (as stated by the 1989 Children Act (Great Britain) and reinforced by subsequent childcare legislation). This brings to the forefront a fundamental issue which is that of your own attitude to inquiry and your participants. Before embarking on your study the examples indicate that it is worth spending some time thinking about your attitude to research and to your participants. For example, when researching with children, are you researching about children or with children? Christensen and Prout's (2002) notion of ethical symmetry is relevant here. They argue that the ethical relationship between researching with adults and children is the same as children are powerful social actors and experts on their own lives. This does not mean that adults and children are treated in the same way but that the most appropriate methods for each group or participant need to be found. This is discussed in some depth by Punch (2002: 338) who states that 'it is too simplistic to consider research with children as one of two extremes: either the same or different from adults. Instead it should be seen as on a continuum where the way that research with children is perceived moves back and forth along the continuum according to a variety of factors: individual children, the questions asked, the research context, whether they are younger or older children and the researcher's own attitudes and behavior with adults'. It may well be that you wish to demonstrate the power of the child's voice within your project or that you wish to observe what children are doing or how they are acting in relation to a particular subject or issue. How you approach this requires some planning and thinking through the implications and potential consequences, and being clear about why you are doing this and what you hope to achieve. As Lambert and Glacken (2011) assert, this reflexive approach requires consideration of how you see children and childhood and the influence that this has on how you approach your research.

 Spending some time considering your own value base as an early years practitioner is useful to analyse how this will influence your approach to your participants and influence your research design. Articulating this within your study will assure the reader that you have an ethically sound basis for your project.

Researching with children

Ethical consent for researching with young children can be a complex area and it is recommended that reading around this subject is undertaken in preparation (Harcourt et al., 2011). It is a powerful argument that children should be seen as capable, competent researchers and participants (Clarke, 2005, Dockett et al., 2009; Harcourt et al., 2011).

When considering your research plan it is essential to think through carefully what your intentions are in respect of involving children and how you plan to ensure their consent in observations, discussions and tasks. There are no easy answers to this. What is important is that you have thought about the nature of their participation within the context of their situation and the scope of your inquiry, consulted with others and reflected this in your written submission.

In view of this it is worth considering the range and time limitations of your inquiry. For example, are you a student already working in a setting where you have established trusting relationships with children or will you be going into placement for a relatively short period of time in order to research? The way that you design and carry out your inquiry will need to take account of the extent you are planning to involve children and how you will explain your work to them and negotiate their agreement through-out the process. Agreement may take the form of assent rather than consent, as babies and very young children are unlikely to be in a position to offer informed consent. Assent is defined as 'agreement by minors who have no legal right to consent' (Alderson and Morrow, 2011: 103). However, as they explain, it is a difficult term which they do not recommend using for three reasons: children who can make informed decisions are consenting not assenting; children who can give partial consent are not consenting or assenting; and children who are not refusing to participate may not feel able to refuse or may be ignored by the researcher. It is worthwhile thinking through these considerations and making a decision about whether the children you are researching with can give consent.

Flewett (2005: 556), in her research with 3-year-old children, found that they were able to give and withdraw consent as she examined their understanding at home and in pre-school during their first year of attendance. She came to this conclusion as they were able to discuss the research with her and ask pertinent questions. She has coined the term 'provisional consent' which is built upon sensitive and trusting collaboration with children. It is described as children's agreement being 'provisional upon the research being conducted within a negotiated, broadly outlined framework and continuing to develop within the participants' expectations'.

Consent should not be assumed but needs negotiation almost on an ongoing basis. It may well be that if you are not in a placement long enough to establish the trusting relationships that are needed to effectively engage with the children, you will need to consider if involving them directly is ethically sensitive. If you decide to involve them as participants you will need to justify your reasons for your decisions about gaining their consent or assent. As Lambert and Glacken (2011) point out, making decisions about whether children are consenting or assenting to the research is mainly assessed by you as the researcher. In order to manage this for the care and safety of children, reading about the subject, using critical friends and tutors as well as your university ethics committee and explaining how you have gone about this in your study are all essential factors.

Harriet obtains the consent of the parents to observe the children which is good practice and indeed a legal requirement in Scandinavia and Australia (Callan et al., 2011). However, she asks herself if this is sufficient, which underpins her view that children are potentially vulnerable, yet capable participants: a view supported by Mukherji and Albon (2010). She talks to the children in simple terms about her research and gains their assent through this process which she finds challenging but an essential part of her practice.

Although this approach may be time-consuming and challenging, it is worth considering the richer information and data that will come from the children themselves as long as care is taken to ensure their consent/ assent is apparent at all times. Babies and children are less complicated than adults who might feel pressurised into complying with the research. Instead children will show obvious signs that they are not happy with their participation, for example, by walking away from you, crying and showing signs of discomfort, or simply by telling you to 'go away'. It is important to be alert to the cues and to ensure children are comfortable with your inquiry processes by checking with them frequently.

It is worth spending time thinking through your proposed research methods with children and anticipating any potential pitfalls. For example, if you are observing children are you a participant observer or a detached observer? What will you do if a child asks you to join in their play while you are observing and how will you manage this situation? What if a child walks away during the observation – are they withdrawing consent, should you follow them? Other areas for consideration may include making sure children are comfortable where you are working with them and managing the potential for them to wish to please you and say what they think you want to hear. In addition there are the needs of children who are not part of your inquiry and how they might feel and whether or not the children have been part of other work-based inquiry and how the experience was for them (Dockett et al., 2009).

Parents can play an important part within the study as their participation can help you to see *where* a child may not be consenting or may have concerns about participation. They can help to frame your inquiry within the needs and understanding of their child and can help in shaping how you carry out the inquiry. Parents are often a neglected source of information and their participation is frequently limited to asking for consent to work with their child. It is worth considering developing relationships with the parents whereby they can play an active role and add an extra dimension to your data. They can provide a sounding board for your ethical considerations where you can put your mind at ease about your ethical conduct.

Protecting yourself

How to protect yourself and others against over involvement, causing potential harm is a question that the students have resolved in different ways. Emily, for example has referred to guidance as a form of support and protection and Harriet has discussed the role of the gatekeeper. Both have used literature and theory to support their stance and actions.

Guidance

There are several guidance documents that can help. Emily, for example, discusses the British Educational Research Association (BERA) guidelines (2011) and this is an essential tool to consult when planning and carrying out the inquiry. We can add to this the British Association for Early Childhood *Code of Ethics* (2011). This takes an approach reflected in Harriet's discussion of 'trust' in her relationships with participants and has a section specifically relating to students. Similarly, the Australian code of ethics (Early Childhood Australia Inc., 2010) and the Scottish Educational Research Association (SERA) 2005 are worth consulting.

University code of ethics

The examples will have taken account of the University code of ethics requirements and will have completed appropriate ethical clearance forms which act as a starting point for your ethical thinking before embarking on your project. This will enable you, in discussion with your tutors, to tease out some of the important issues before you begin.

Harriet talks about having to negotiate with a 'gatekeeper', a term that has classically been used within social inquiry. It usually refers to a manager or leader in a setting who oversees the remit of the inquiry and can allow access to the setting and the participants. Harriet describes in detail the role she asked her gatekeeper to play in gaining consent from participants and in ensuring that this was carried out with the greatest ethical propriety possible, within the scope of the participant inquiry. This implies that the gatekeeper plays a formal role in ensuring that all involved will be protected. In Chapter 5, Nikki questions the term 'gatekeeper', as she feels it resembles a castle where access is restricted and has sought to find another term. Nikki chooses to use the term 'research activator' to describe a person who ensures that the research causes no harm to participants.

Although practitioner research does require careful negotiation, honesty and respect, which Harriet and Nikki clearly demonstrate, the terms 'gatekeeper' and 'research activator' are actually at odds with the approach that we believe should be taken to such inquiry. If we are looking at study as being *with* participants and not *on* them, then the term 'gatekeeper', so frequently used by students, becomes null and void. It is a term which very much reflects an 'us and them' approach to inquiry; it assumes that there are barriers between researcher and participant that need to be infiltrated. This does not apply if research is approached collaboratively within a setting.

It is far more helpful to consider forming research partnerships: who are the people around you who will help to support you and help you manage your inquiry? This will, in all likelihood, include someone in a professional or management role who can take a lead within the setting, enabling you to gain access and consent for your work. But much more than just providing access, they can give you valuable advice on your approach and the feasibility of your inquiry within that particular setting. This person can help you in modifying the approaches that you take, through their knowledge and under-standing of how your project will work within the context of their setting. It may be someone who will help you to negotiate barriers as well as provide a safety net for all concerned. In this way they are an invaluable partner in your inquiry, rather than the foreboding obstacle that 'gatekeeper' implies.

 Contrary to the popular view of research as an isolated activity, it is also helpful to find a critical friend who can discuss and tease out issues with you. Far from being a cosy relationship, this should be someone who you feel safe enough with to enable you to look at experimenting, taking risks and explor-ing within safe boundaries. They can often see new perspectives, give ideas and question your thinking – having your best interests at the heart of their queries. Several critical friends can help in terms of piloting your questionnaires or interviews, for example, to ensure these frame your questions in the best way possible both to meet the needs of the data you wish to gather and the needs of respondents.

How should ethics 'look' within your study?

A consideration for your written presentation of your study is whether ethics should form a separate section within your methodology or whether it should thread through your entire work. Certainly, a separate section makes it easier to locate and to provide an overview. However, as this is such an important issue it may be worth considering at every stage. For example, your introduction is likely to contain a rationale for your study where your personal reasons for undertaking the topic you have chosen are explained. Emily has explained her reasons as encompassing her concern at how potential changes in funding could impact on services for children and families. This lends itself to a consideration of the ethics involved in separating out the personal from the professional and in ensuring a boundary between personal feelings and inquiry and the potential for researcher bias contaminating the data. In linking theory to practice and positioning your study within the literature review, you will need to consider the type of literature you are using. Does it reflect a bias to your viewpoint for example? What sort of assumptions are you making about your project and does the literature support these?

The methodology you use to design your inquiry is likely to require that you consider your position within the inquiry either as an insider or outsider or as a *hands on* or *hands off* researcher. Either stance will require you to think through the ethical implications. Similarly, research methods should be designed with the participants' needs in mind. As Harriet has explored, for example, can the participants understand the written material, will she need these translated into the first language of her respondents? Emily decides on recording conversations with a purpose as the best way of ensuring additional stress is not placed on participants already dealing with the sensitive issues involved.

In analysing the findings of your study, discussion of ethics plays a part in evaluating the transparency of your inquiry, from the language you use to explain your findings, to the honesty with which you represent your data in order to make a contribution to the field of knowledge in your subject area.

Finally, within the consideration of ethics comes the importance of finishing your work positively for all concerned. Respecting participants' contributions involves thought around feeding back to them about your findings and what you intend to do with these. It also involves expressing a thank you as well as considering the implications of relationships formed during the process and how these should be ended appropriately or whether they will be continued. It is all too easy to be swept up in completing the work by deadlines and to forget our obligations to those who have helped and supported our inquiry. This is considered more fully in Chapter 9.

Taken as a whole, your dissertation is a research story which exhibits 'your commitment to criticality, demonstrating its authenticity, rigour and scholarship' (McNiff and Whitehead, 2011: 166). You share your knowledge so others can benefit from it and positive outcomes for children and families can be achieved. Through their writing both Emily and Harriet have demonstrated the dispositions we would expect from an early years practitioner as a professional and a researcher. Children and families deserve our wholehearted commitment to their well-being. This means taking the time to understand the needs of participants and in planning and thinking through your approach using the support of the research partners around you.

Key points from the chapter

- Building trusting relationships with participants are key to developing a sound ethical basis to your study.

- Researching *with* and not *on* participants is a fundamental part of ensuring your stance is ethical.

- Establishing and articulating your position as an insider or outsider to the setting and understanding the implications of this for your participants is an important part of your study.

- Careful planning of your actions in respect of researching with children is needed to ensure that they assent and are partners within your research.

- Using guidance, codes of practice, theory, literature and partnerships with the team around you as a student can act as a protection and an underpinning for your work.

Further reading

Alderson, P. and Morrow, V. (2011) *The Ethics of Research with Children and Young People: A Practical Handbook.* London: Sage.
This is a practical book which gives guidance on laws, guidelines and current debates about ethicality in researching with young people and children.

Harcourt, D., Perry, B. and Waller, T. (2011) *Researching Young Children's Perspectives.* Oxford: Routledge.
Using case studies, this book considers the challenges and complexities in researching with children, exploring the values and principles which inform ethical practice within early childhood research. Discussion and reflection on issues promotes confidence in researching within this area.

Lambert, V. and Glacken, M. (2011) Engaging with children in research: theoretical and practical implications of negotiating informed consent/assent, *Nursing Ethics*, 18: 781–801.
This article provides useful information and examples in talking to children about research.

Punch, S. (2002) Research with children: the same or different as research with adults? *Childhood*, 9: 321–41.
This article discusses the challenges and strengths in gathering data with children.

4 Literature review

This chapter:
- Evaluates the importance of the literature review;
- Demonstrates the ability to build an argument, making links between literature and your topic;
- Shows how to position your research as a result of the review;
- Explains the review as an ongoing process within your inquiry;
- Discusses the importance of reflection on the process as well as on the content of the review.

Introduction

Students often ask whether they need to do a literature review at all as it may influence their thinking about the subject before they have researched it and may lead to foregone conclusions or pre-empting the findings. However, as Chapter 1 demonstrates, your research question is likely to be framed within the context of something you know. You may be influenced by personal experience, the media, your own knowledge and discussions with others. These are likely to be contributing factors to your choice of question. The critical issue, Haverkamp and Young (2007: 285) suggest is not what you already know about the subject but how you use this to design your research: 'The goal is to become familiar with the background literature without becoming tied to or directed by particular theories or models'. Trying to keep an open mind can be challenging and this is where the skill of being a reflective practitioner as an early years professional will help you to look at the literature through different lenses. This chapter explores and evaluates Leanne's literature review in terms of how she presents her study focus on improving her understanding of child-initiated learning.

When Leanne explains the type and scope of the literature she intends to use (below), she enables the reader to put the topic into perspective and to see how she frames her review in light of relevant sources. Reflecting on and explaining your rationale for including certain sources and theory helps the reader to see how you have focused your search. Your review will expand the reader's knowledge and will serve as an underpinning base whereby the reader is given confidence that you understand your subject and are aware of the key texts. Therefore, you can be seen as a credible source of information and a researcher who adds to the existing pool of knowledge about your subject. This will aid the reliability and validity of your research which is discussed further in Chapter 6.

Leanne starts her review by saying that:

> Brookfield (1995) suggests that when we investigate an area of our practice we should look at it from the theoretical perspective. McNiff and Whitehead (2009) point out that with action research projects a literature review is not necessary but as a practitioner researcher I need to engage with the thinking of different theorists in order to evaluate the validity of my own ideas in comparison with theirs. This section of my study analyses the theory related to my issue. It focuses on the four main points that were identified in the introduction to the study.

Commentary

In her introduction, Leanne poses her question '**How can I improve my knowledge of child initiated learning and feel more confident facilitating it in a reception class?**'.

From this she outlines four key points of study:

- What actually is child initiated learning?

- How should practitioners facilitate self directed learning?

- What percentage of the activities in a reception classroom should be child initiated?

- How does effective leadership initiate change and improvement associated with pedagogical issues?

She has considered these questions through her reading and in discussion with others to narrow down a potentially wide research area to fit the scope of her study. This is one way of getting started with your review: beginning with a broad perspective of the literature and taking a funnelling approach to narrowing this down to key specific areas within your topic. Leanne has used these as headings to effectively divide her work and to keep focused within the scope of her project.

Leanne's introduction to her literature review may have started you thinking about why we should do a literature review at all and what purpose it should serve within your study. She sets out her reasons for doing the review. It may well be that you agree with Leanne's reasons or that you have reasons of your own; either way it is important to make these clear to the reader so that they can understand your approach and why you have chosen the sources you have used. The model in Figure 4.1 highlights many of the reasons for doing a literature review and there is one blank space for you to add your own.

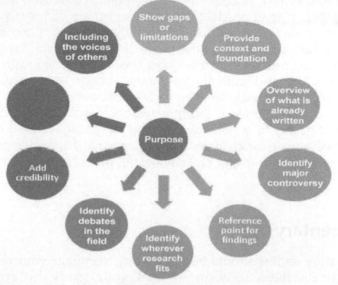

Figure 4.1 Reasons for doing a literature review

Key points for you to consider are that: the review should identify a gap that your research can fill, justify why your research is worth doing and explain your motivation for undertaking it.

 If we consider research design as similar to purchasing a house, you will be unlikely to choose your house without considering how the other houses in the street look, the area that it is in and any structures around the house – connections to the mains water supply, telephone, preservation orders and so on that you have to take into account. When considering your literature review you will need to think about what other debates around your subject include, whether these include disagreements within the issue and the context surrounding the subject. In designing your research, consideration of the existing theories and literature surrounding the subject will influence how you approach its design. Just like you would only decide to purchase a house having considered a number of external factors, you should only clarify a research question having considered the existing body of knowledge in this area.

Leanne sets out clearly what she intends to consider in her literature review.

She writes:

> My research begins by explaining my background, my rationale and my perspective of the issue. It then examines the theoretical views which discuss the four key points considered above. Significant views on child initiated learning are compared and contrasted. The review focuses on early pioneers' opinions on education and discusses the views of relevant child development theorists and identifies how their theories link with my issue. Past and current government policy and legislative frameworks are included. The theory associated with leadership and change models is incorporated because issues that need investigating in a setting may lead to change and quality improvement for children. I reflect on what I have identified from the literature and explain how this may change my views.

Commentary

The literature review should be a good way to engage your reader early and motivate them to want to read your study by arguing the importance or need for your research.

Leanne has chosen a topic about which there is a wealth of material and information, and it can be daunting to decide how to choose what is important and relevant. As Leanne had identified four main areas for her research she was able to narrow her search using key words and phrases such as 'child initiated learning' and 'self directed learning'. Defining key vocabulary and key terms is a good starting point to begin your search for literature. Leanne has selected sources by putting these into search engines offered through her library and the internet and library resources. Bell (1988), writing from a student's perspective, suggests following three criteria when accessing sources: deciding which type of literature to use; which key terms to search; and identifying a time span during which the research should concentrate. This gives a systematic approach to the review, which is important in terms of giving rigour to the study. However, the review should go further than summarising the sources, but afford opportunities to generate new ideas and new directions for the field of your research. As Beth, a student quoted by Fleer and Barker (2008: 80) says: 'long before you start the literature review you understand that you need to "sing a new song" when piecing it together'.

In order to select the most relevant sources to consider, it is worth thinking through the process used by an early years practitioner to develop children's learning. To start with, the practitioner promotes curiosity and interest in children by providing a choice of a number of resources and possible lines of inquiry that she thinks might be relevant to the area of interest. She listens to the child's voice and observes closely what the child is interested in within the topic and plans how to incorporate this interest into the child's day. She then plans the next steps and reviews progress. Doing a literature review is not dissimilar in terms of starting out with a wide range of sources or choices, closely looking at these to establish which are of most interest to your topic, listening to the voices of others in the field, incorporating these into planning your review and continually reviewing progress.

Leanne starts with her first question:

What is child initiated learning?

Froebel (cited in Lawrence, 1952) and Montessori (1988) both valued child initiated activity and agreed that children are able to motivate themselves to learn when they are given ownership of the learning process and able to make their own decisions. These early educational pioneers saw the benefits of this type of learning but through the years there has been some confusion as to what child initiated activity actually means. **Often certain practitioners who teach older children think that child initiated learning is just a posh way of saying play. To a certain extent they are correct and in agreement is the Department for Children, Schools and Families (DCSF, England, 2009) who tell us that child initiated activity has many features that are similar to play. But purposeful play is important and essential in children's learning.** The new Early Years Framework from the Department for Education (DfE, 2012, England) informs us that children discover new concepts by directing their own play. The same view is shared by Clarke (2008) who believes that children learn by experiencing activities that they have freely chosen. Pritchard (2009) concurs and points out that learners need to be involved and engage with a new idea or experience in an active way to enable them to understand it. When children play with objects and use their senses to discover new information this is how new connections are made in the brain. Child initiated activities are the vital link between play and learning.

Continues

Continued

Fisher (2002) states that child initiated activity allows children to make their own choices in their learning, by deciding what equipment they need and which methods they will use to reach their end result. The DCSF (2008) defines child initiated learning as a child becoming absorbed in something that they have selected. However they also add other elements to this type of learning. It can be where a child uses an object for a different function than intended. They then take the lead and turn the purpose of the play to suit their thoughts, feelings and actions. Bruce (2004) discusses the theorist Piaget who refers to this as symbolic representation where children have their own individual ideas and use them to make something represent something else. For example a child could be stirring a muddle puddle with a stick and saying this is yummy soup. However the practitioner may have planned for the child to pretend to write letters using the stick as a pencil. Another form of child initiated learning highlighted by the DCSF (2008) is concerned with supporting children's interests. A pupil may bring in an object from home or share an experience that they have had with the adult and the class.

 What is your opinion on Leanne's use of language within this section? For example, I have highlighted in bold where she talks about the view that child-initiated learning is just a 'posh way of saying play'. Should she be using more academic language in a research project?

Commentary

Within this section, Leanne has carefully thought through her use of sources, including the time span she is including in her review. She has considered the current policy context in looking at the revised Early Years Foundation Stage (EYFS) (DfE, 2012) and has referred to earlier versions of EYFS (DCSF, 2008) and government guidance. This is important as it shows that you are considering the context of your topic and showing understanding of how early years practice has reached the point it is now at in terms of government thinking. When deciding on what legislation, policy and guidance framework to refer to, it is necessary to use judgement in how far to go back in time in explaining policy and what is relevant to include. While it is important to show you understand the history of your topic, if using older material it is important to explain why you are using this and its relevance to your research question, thus justifying its inclusion. Also, if you are using information that is integral to your research question, make sure you have the most up-to-date information possible. For example, if you are researching about the cultural make-up of an area, ensure that you are using the most up-to-date census information available.

As you can see from Leanne's review, she has allowed the reader to hear her voice and you are in no doubt that she is telling the story as she sees it, using the literature to support her. I have highlighted within the excerpt in bold where Leanne's voice indicates her thinking on the issues.

In order to achieve the credibility and authenticity discussed above and in Chapter 6, you will need to do more than explain the literature. You will need to show that you can apply it to practice, be critical in your approach, make your own interpretation clear, compare and contrast, make connections between literature and your own research, and build an argument. Leanne has managed this within this short excerpt. In her discussion about the nature of child-initiated play, she has been able to synthesise her work by breaking down the material and rebuilding it to form a new entity. She has made the theory more accessible to the reader by doing this and by relating her material directly to practice, as suggested by Punch (1995). In the words of Torraco (2005: 359), she has synthesised by 'weaving core streams of research together to focus on core issues and produces a new model' and by doing this shows the reader her 'intimate knowledge of the subject'. This again adds to the reader's perception of the reliability of your work.

Leanne is helped in this by having a variety of sources on which to draw, including theorists, books and government guidance, and she could have added journals, websites, newspaper articles and other research in the field. Peer-reviewed articles contain valuable sources of knowledge as they are a method of keeping track of new knowledge in the field, and each article will have been scrutinised by experts who have contributed new knowledge themselves and who will have reviewed the paper for originality and robustness. These provide up-to-date and credible information. While using a variety of sources to give a well-rounded review, make sure that these are credible sources. In terms of websites, check if these have been used within your local or university library resources, as librarians will have evaluated these for suitability. Look to see who wrote the web page and if they refer to credible authors. Consider the view that the website offers; for example, a government website will be likely to provide the party view and you may need to look to other sources for critiques. Be wary of websites that are actually selling a product (for example, a particular phonics scheme) and so extol the virtues of it in a biased way. Check to see if the website has up-to-date information. If in doubt ask your librarian, who will be able to provide a wealth of knowledge and support. Ensure that websites relate to your topic; for example, if researching about safeguarding children in

Great Britain be wary about using websites from other countries where the data refers to that country.

 Setting your topic within the context of the wider socio-political context will help the reader position your research. For example, if looking at healthy eating within a setting, discussing some of the impact of policy issues on family life will illuminate the wider dilemmas rather than highlight the fact that some children's lunchboxes contain unhealthy food. Demonstrate that you have taken the time to research, for example, the fact that families living in areas of deprivation may be less likely to have access to a local shop selling reasonable priced choices of fruit and vegetables and other healthy food, and that they are less likely to have transport to supermarkets or shops selling healthier food. This shows that you have a deeper understanding of some of the issues behind the topic you are presenting and have been able to analyse some of the challenges and dilemmas within these.

Leanne continues to write:

How can practitioners facilitate and support child initiated learning in their classrooms?

According to Waller (2009) practitioners should observe and record children's actions in their free play. This will then help them to identify what is appealing to each child. In agreement with this view is Lindon (2010) who advises practitioners to concentrate on becoming aware of and following what has engaged a child's interest. Regular observations help practitioners decide the next steps. Samuelsson and Carlsson (2008) inform us that play is initiated by children and learning is initiated by adults. Clarke (2008) would argue that practitioners plan activities using information from observations of self directed activity and can then modify them. Children are then able to learn new concepts through their play that extend their knowledge.

Sometimes observations alone do not provide enough information. The DCSF (2008) informs practitioners of the need to carry out more detailed observations where they talk to and work with individuals or groups in the class to obtain more evidence. This is similar to the Effective Provision of Pre-School Education [EPPE] Report (Sylva et al., 2004) which identified that effective early years educators interact with children using the sustained shared thinking technique examined by Siraj-Blatchford (2007). With this method the practitioner and child or group can work together to solve problems or clarify a concept. This approach would be particularly useful to assess children's understanding and developmental levels.

Fisher (2002) emphasises the need for children's surroundings to be interesting, exciting and stimulating. They will then want to explore and discover what is available to them. Featherstone and Bayley (2006) strongly believe that the environment should be the 'third teacher'. The layout should be inviting, informative and fun. The resources should be clearly labelled and easily accessible. This then promotes independence because children are able to find items and return them to the correct place.

The DfE (2012) say that Early Years workers should respond to each child's interests and requirements. When children bring in items from home to 'show and tell' or discuss activities that they have participated in practitioners need to support children's development by showing enthusiasm and interest.

Commentary

Leanne extends her range of literature here to include the EPPE (Sylva et al., 2004) research and skilfully weaves sources together with her own experience and opinions to look at key concepts surrounding her topic. For example, using observations to gauge children's interests, to ascertain child led play and to inform next steps for the child, including the use of sustained shared thinking as a tool to develop shared learning.

Leanne uses a number of relevant references to support her work. Quotations are helpful to use but ensure that quotes are short and to the point as the reader will want to hear your voice rather than the voices of theorists and long quotes add little value to your work.

It is useful here to think about how your research fits into the literature and how it will inform practice. This means that your review will need to be ongoing throughout the research. It is not a chapter you can do and then leave with a sigh of relief when it is done. New ideas within your subject are likely to be developing all the time and it is useful to keep up to date with new publications, perhaps through email alerts from your library database. Also, as your research progresses, you may reflect and review at each point and find that your literature needs adjusting in the light of new findings. One way of keeping this in the forefront is to consider making a grid or quadrant in which you can keep a track of your literature as you go along and keep making connections to your study.

One example of this might be as in Figure 4.2.

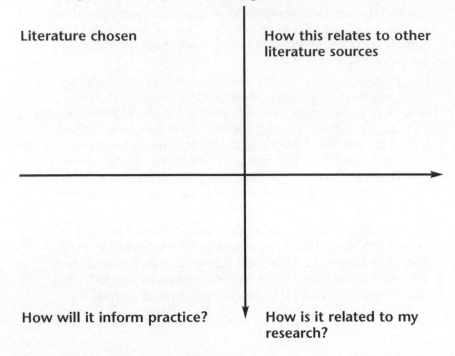

Figure 4.2 Comparing and contrasting literature sources 1

Similarly, see Table 4.1.

4.1 Comparing and contrasting literature sources 2

	Source 1	Source 2
Reference	Fisher 2002	Featherstone and Bailey 2006
How does it connect to my research?	Discusses the importance of an enabling environment to facilitate child-initiated play. Develops argument about practitioners' role in facilitating child-initiated play	Gives a strong message about the importance of the environment
Is there a quote I can use? Pg no.		Cites Malaguzzi in environment being the 'third teacher'
Why is it useful?	Positions the research in under-standing how practitioners can facilitate child-initiated play	This strengthens the review by looking at a holistic approach to child-initiated play
Do I agree/disagree?	Supports my argument	Supports my argument
What are the strengths and key contribution of piece of literature?	Develops thinking in that observations recording, assessment and practitioner interaction with children may not be enough to fully develop child-initiated play.	Develops this strongly to support child's independence which demonstrates the value of child-initiated play
What comparisons/contrasts can be made?		These sources support and build on each other

This type of grid allows you to see at a glance how your sources compare with each other and each source's contribution to the whole. Recording your literature searches in such a systematic way will enable you to demonstrate rigour within the study, the importance of which is discussed in Chapter 6. Once you have gathered sources, these will need to be presented as a coherent section, not just a summary of each one. The reader should be able to see that your research is worthwhile and to be clear about what you are researching. At first, you may begin with a broad brush of ideas, like a fisherman casting a net into the sea to see what can be caught, but in using the grids and structuring and synthesising information you may move towards a more detailed discussion of a few specific ideas or texts. As Leanne has done, you can synthesise a number of key texts in one paragraph, including you own interpretation and opinions on the issue. It is worth remembering that the number of sources used is less important than the quality, the relevance and how you have organised them.

 Referencing as you go along is vital as from experience, I have spent many hours trying to locate a reference I have used but not written down properly at the time. The temptation is to think that you will remember it and that it is more important to put your thoughts down and not interrupt the flow of your work, but in practice pausing to note the reference is far less time consuming and avoids the disappointment of not being able to use it because you cannot find it again.

In the next excerpt, Leanne explores a dilemma which has been discussed by theorists and professionals alike in relation to her topic. She presents the arguments in readiness for further exploration in her setting:

What percentage of activities should be child initiated?

There still remains some confusion as to what percentage of activities in a setting should provide opportunities for child initiated learning. The literature search has not presented an actual percentage. EPPE (Sylva et al., 2004) recommends that practitioners in a reception class should work towards an equal balance of child initiated and adult led activities. However they also add that nearly half of the self directed incidents included interventions from practitioners to extend the learning process and enabled adults to plan teacher led activities based on their observations. Bennett et al. (2001: 33) refer to this as children 'setting the agenda'. This demonstrates how the curriculum can be guided by children's free choice activities.

The DCSF (2008) and the new guidance in the DfE (2012)

Continues

Continued

make it clear that practitioners should use their own experience and knowledge of each child in their setting to decide what the appropriate balance should be. The same view is shared by Fisher (2002) who adds that this judgement can change from day to day and session to session. She believes that younger children need more child initiated activity. The DfE (2012) in the new early years framework also present this idea, they suggest that more adult led activities should take place towards the end of the reception year to prepare children for more formal lessons in year one. The DCSF (2009) argue that this depends more on development level and personal preferences than age. A child in nursery may prefer more structure whereas a child in a reception class may decide to choose more child initiated activity.

Commentary

Your project may raise more questions than you started with, which will add to your body of knowledge as new questioning leads to new ideas and learning. Listening to the voices of those most involved with your subject will enable you to determine your approach as new questions emerge which will shape your project. As Costley et al. (2010: 14) point out: 'As a work based researcher you already have a level of knowledge about your area of work' and comprehensive knowledge of the work-based context. Thus you are the expert and should use your own experience when selecting literature sources. In this way Leanne knows that important sources for her work are the Department for Education, for example, but that her search for a percentage figure for the balance of child-led and adult-led activities is perhaps not one that can or should be answered.

Leanne goes on to consider her fourth question:

How does effective leadership initiate change and improvement associated with pedagogical issues?

Reed and Canning (2012) tell us that early years practitioners are continually planning ways to change and improve certain areas of practice. McNiff et al. (2003) believe that all staff employed in the early years should become active change agents. She also reminds us that everyday changes that appear to be trivial can make amendments to the big change picture. For change to be successful there needs to be a lead professional who can act as an agent of change and motivate and inspire others to follow (Rodd, 2006). Chapman's (2011) view is slightly different as he emphasises the need for leaders to discuss the process with everyone involved. Sharing this view is Preedy et al. (2003) who says that staff experiencing change must be aware why the amendments are necessary and should be allowed to contribute to any discussions. This would be beneficial in my setting because there are many practitioners who would like to share ideas and discuss strategies. However Askew and Carnell (1998) emphasise that change only happens when practitioners understand the values and principles of their colleagues and why they choose to behave the way they do.

Examining issues from the theoretical viewpoint has increased my understanding of child initiated learning and has answered some of my key points in my introduction. It has now prompted some questions in relation to my own practice which are:

- Are all practitioners clear of what child initiated learning is?

- Do we facilitate it appropriately in our setting?

- Do practitioners adequately cater for the needs of all children in the setting?

- Can early years practitioners initiate change through work based inquiry?

Some of these questions are included in my questionnaires and discussed later in my study.

Commentary

Here Leanne discusses how the literature and theoretical aspects included in her review have influenced the questions she needs to ask in relation to her own practice, and the gaps in knowledge which position her research. Not only has she refined her questions but she has also used the review to inform her data collection methods. This shows clearly the thought process of her work and a holistic approach to the project in that each section of the research has informed the others and been informed in its turn.

Leanne completes this section of her work with a reflection on the work she has done within the review. She writes:

Reflection part 1

By examining the literature I became more aware of the pedagogical approaches associated with child initiated learning.
The theory has given me suggestions on how to facilitate this
learning style in my workplace. Some of the ideas recommended in the literature were occurring on a regular basis in
my setting but I often took these observations for granted. By
taking a step back and questioning my practice I have developed a more profound understanding of why this type of
learning is so important. Bolton (2010) refers to this type of
reflection as going 'through the mirror' where I have extended
my personal and professional knowledge of an issue. Events
and actions that happened on a daily basis took on new meaning because I looked at them from a different angle and in
more detail. In order to start the journey of changing aspects
of my practice I needed to follow Brookfield's (1995) suggestion of gaining the views of my colleagues and the children in
my setting to see if we cater for the needs of all children and
to comment on how their views compare or contrast with the
literature.

Commentary

This demonstrates the impact the literature review has had on Leanne
before she started choosing her approach and data collection. Looking at
the literature in this way has enabled her to identify how this relates to
practice and to take a step back to observe and reflect on this. She sets the
literature review into the context of her research in now seeing how
others view the topic. This gives roundedness to the research study and
adds to the credibility and authentic nature of the research. Explaining
and reflecting on the use and justification of literature is an important
consideration not just within the literature review but in all the different
parts of the research. As Tummers and Karsten (2011) point out, it is
important to explain how literature is used within your study as it will
give the reader an understanding of how existing theories are managed
in the design of your research and how you have carried it out. Through
examining examples of public administration research, Tummers and
Karsten (2011) have been able to identify opportunities and pitfalls in the
use of literature within each research activity: research design, data
collection and data analysis. Within research design, such opportunities
and pitfalls include the ability to identify gaps in knowledge, identifying
its relevance and to focus the research. However, there is a danger that
relevant theory may be overlooked in that the impact of theory you have
read may divert you from other emerging considerations. The value of

Leanne's reflections here are in enabling such consideration to take place. You should compare your data to the key points which arose within your literature review, but be careful not to only focus on these and lose sight of other important findings that have emerged through your data. Within data analysis, use of literature can enhance insight but equally can impose a predetermined understanding of findings. This will be considered more fully in Chapter 7.

 Key points from the chapter

Consider and explain within your project when you will use literature and for what purpose, and how you will reflect upon its value and potential limiting factors:

- Reflect on and explain the reason why you have chosen your literature sources.

- Consider the time frame for the inclusion of literature.

- Try to identify a gap that your research can fill or explain how your research is positioned within the available knowledge about the subject.

- Use a funnel approach in starting with a broad perspective and funnelling down to the most relevant sources for your study.

- Continue to review the literature section in the light of your emerging research.

Further reading

Aveyard, H. (2010) *Doing A Literature Review in Health and Social Care.* 2nd edn. Maidenhead: McGraw-Hill.
Although aimed at health and social care professionals, this book provides a clear step-by-step guide which relates to all fields of research.

Hart, C. (2001) *Doing a Literature Search – a Comprehensive Guide for the Social Sciences.* London: Sage.
A really helpful, straightforward guide to planning and conducting a literature search, including advice on how to identify key themes in the literature.

Jesson, J.K., Matheson, L. and Lacey, F.M. (2011) *Doing Your Literature Review.* London: Sage.
This book is aimed at a wide spectrum of students and takes you through a clear guide to doing a systematic review.

5 Methodology: choosing your research approach

This chapter:

- Discusses an exciting part of your research design where you are shaping your approach into a set of ideas and theories that fit your context, how you see the topic and your needs as a researcher;
- Helps you to really focus on what you want to discover in doing your project;
- Explores the values, knowledge and principles that underpin your project;
- Gives you advice on how to construct your research design.

Introduction

Deciding an approach (or research methodology) is an integral part of research design and should be distinguished from your choice of methods of collecting data. Without making a distinction between your approach or methodology and your methods (the data collection tools that you use, for example, questionnaires), the research design will be weakened and your findings less robust. This could be illustrated by the example of building a house. If all of the builders came to the site with their tools and materials but no plans, they could attempt to build the house, however, without the architect's design it would be likely to fall down. Choosing an approach can be a confusing part of your study in that there is not an 'off the peg' approach that you can easily adopt as suitable for your research design; you have to construct it. This means some reading, reflection and borrowing of ideas from different sources to construct an approach which fits your ideas for research and the context in which it will be carried out. Or alternatively you could start with an established methodology and choose methods which allow you to feel comfortable about your ethical stance. This can be an exciting part of your research design as you can shape your approach into a paradigm (or set of ideas and theories) that fit your context. How you see the topic and your needs as a researcher can help you to really focus on what you want to discover in your work-based inquiry and influence how you should go about it.

Constructing your research paradigm requires you to question your way of viewing the world; to consider the assumptions you make about understanding the world around you and the values and beliefs that you hold. These beliefs will have a significant influence upon the decisions that you make in choosing between research approaches. When you select methods to go about gathering your data, this selection and combination of approaches will assist you in assuring the credibility of your research. Denzin (2006) discussed the concept of triangulation whereby different methods and ways of collecting data enable contrast and comparison and support your findings to give credibility and robustness to your study. Triangulating your approaches will further strengthen your research design so that the results of the research can be seen to be credible. This is considered more fully in Chapter 6.

When considering your approach, it is a good idea to start with your interests and purpose in undertaking the research and to think about what information it will be most valuable for you to collect. Just as we considered in Chapter 1, you need to consider the following questions: how will the research improve your knowledge? How will it improve your practice and potentially, practice at your setting? What is it you really want to know about or change? Thinking through the context of where you are researching may be helpful; in doing this, you will begin to understand what the relationship is between your research and your own professional development. Are you carrying out the research in a real-world situation, perhaps in a setting or your workplace? And what types of approaches lend themselves to this? How will your findings continue to be part of your professional practice after the study is completed? When telling 'the story' of your research process, that is, writing up your research as a study, it should demonstrate how the research has illuminated your learning process and enriched your own understanding of your practice. Your motivation is important in undertaking the inquiry as this will lend a criticality to your work as you focus on what is not right and could be better within your practice. 'The why of the research is vital' (Solvason, 2011: 35). This is your chance to make a difference to practice and to improve outcomes for the children in your care and their families.

Nikki explains how she has constructed her approach:

Having made a decision on the area of research I wanted to investigate, my first step was to identify a person who could grant permission for carrying out the research, Denscombe (2007: 71) identifies this person as the 'gatekeeper' and states that 'seeking the permission of gatekeepers ... is often an unavoidable first step in gaining access to data'. Whilst I would agree with Denscombe (2007) that this is the first step for a researcher to take, I did not like the term gatekeeper. I decided to use the term 'Research Activator' (R.A.) as to me it is an explicit link to the research and did not conjure up the image of someone guarding a castle. The R.A. in this study was the manager of the Sure Start Children's Centre where I work.

Once the R.A. had granted permission as a researcher I was required to consider which paradigm I would use. I was aware there were a number of paradigms available and believed selecting one would be a simple task, yet the reality was it ended up being confusing and complex. Firstly, given that I wanted to look at how the parents perceived both the sessions and how the centre worked in partnership with them, initial thoughts were that my stance would be a phenomenological one. The reason for this was that this approach according to Denscombe (2007: 76) meant that I would be 'seeing things through the eyes of others', and the data I would collect would be collected using audio equipment which further advocated this approach.

At the same time the grounded theory approach seemed relevant too, since the research was small scale; it involved interactions between parents and practitioners; I was a practitioner within the setting. Since both seemed to be relevant to the research I was due to undertake I felt quite apprehensive that the research needed to fit exactly into one approach. However, on further reading I considered the investigation would be most suitable using an action research approach since it demonstrated clearly the four elements specific to action research; **Practical, change, cyclical process and participation.** In terms of practicality my research is aimed at dealing with real-world problems and issues as it is at my workplace. It encompasses change as [a] way of dealing with practical problems and as a means of discovering more about my topic to inform change. As a cyclical process it involves a feedback loop in which initial findings generate possibilities for change which are then implemented and evaluated as a prelude to further investigation. Practitioners as active participants are the crucial people in my research process (Denscombe, 2007).

Action research according to MacNaughton et al. (2001: 210) starts with a wish to 'improve your understandings about why and how something happens'. Whilst Denscombe (2007: 122) acknowledges 'it has a particular niche among professionals who want to use research to improve their practices'. Both theories reflected my reasons since I wanted to look at further developing the existing practices of involving parents in shaping services and that of parents and practitioners working in partnership. Denscombe (2007) acknowledges that action research is a strategy, not a specific method recognised for social research, it does not identify any restrictions regarding the means that can be used for collecting data.

Whilst using the strategy of action research I shall adopt an interpretivist paradigm. The research is based around parents currently attending the Children's Centre where I work and will investigate working in partnership with parents and their involvement in shaping the services that the centre provides. The findings will continue to be part of my professional practice long after the study is handed in. Therefore the interpretivist approach will work best as it is 'particularly relevant when studying anything to do with human society' (Walliman and Buckler, 2008: 162). Similarly, MacNaughton et al. (2001) state that this approach attempts to obtain knowledge of how people comprehend the social world. The data that will be gathered will be that of a qualitative nature which further reinforces the interpretive approach.

Commentary

Nikki has considered several approaches before settling on action research within an interpretivist approach, or paradigm, which she defines as finding out how people see the social world. When you take an interpretivist approach, you accept that there are no set answers to questions that we have – but that individuals will hold their own views. Therefore research is all about finding out what those views are rather than seeking a 'correct' answer. Nikki wishes to find out how parents see the services at the children's centre and if they feel involved in shaping these. She is seeking their views.

There are two key types of action research, one which involves locating an external problem to be solved (for example, parents do not appear to want to be involved in activities at the setting) and one which focuses on self-development. If Nikki had taken the self-development approach, this would have changed her question to 'how do I make parents feel more involved in activities at the setting?'. Instead Nikki's approach fits within the first, more classic, approach to action research.

Nikki discusses some of the approaches she has used to create her research design. What is important is that she has explained her thought processes in doing this and has related the approaches to her own research, explaining where they fit her intentions. She expressed apprehensions about whether it was necessary for her research to fit into one approach. This does not need to be the case as she discusses phenomenology, grounded theory and action research, and uses an interpretive approach within her work and supports this effectively with the use of literature. These are some of the many different approaches that can be used and it is possible to select and combine elements of these as long as you explain why you are choosing them and the reader is in no doubt that you have thought clearly about the issues within your research project.

You may wonder if developing such a wide range of methodological dispositions towards inquiry may lead to confusion or a 'watered down' approach. It may be argued that a stance like Nikki's provides a breadth of views without the necessary depth on which to build an analysis of findings. But on the contrary, the process of Nikki considering where her research fits demonstrates critical thinking on her part as highlighted by Smith et al. (2011) which gives her inquiry richness and depth. Denscombe (2010) sees this as the 'deconstruction' of data where Nikki is constantly questioning herself about her approach and where and how her data collection methods fit her design. As Denscombe suggests, the researcher needs to be active in evaluating and revisiting this. Nikki has achieved this by considering how best to elicit her participants' views within the context of their 'stay and play' sessions. She is 'interrogating' the data, asking herself questions and thinking critically about the originating context of the work. It is through careful consideration that Nikki focuses upon action research as the key strategy within her methodology, as she believes that the four elements specific to action research – practical, change, cyclical process and participation – will effectively underpin her approach. Nikki chooses this as a vehicle for her research as she can see that each of these mirror her intentions for the inquiry.

Spradley (1979) looks at this consideration of context further and suggests the researcher explores the physical environment, the people involved and their aims, the activities that occurred and sequence of events, the key actions that took place and the timescale. It is also worth considering the emotional environment as this is an important aspect to discuss so that the reader can understand where the research is positioned. These are all areas which Nikki as an early years practitioner has thought about in her research design.

There is a danger, however, that such an approach means that you interpret data or situations in a way that mirrors your own perspective and position. Carr (2000) argues that this is not just unavoidable but necessary in that you are undeniably a part of the research. Your experiences and beliefs are central to the research you carry out and this is why it is so important that your reasoning behind your choice of approach is clear for the reader to understand (see Chapter 2 for further discussion). It is because of this that the level of rigour that Nikki demonstrates in her consideration of approaches should be applied when choosing your methodology and that critical reflection and self-reflection (the bedrock of early years professional practice) should be employed. The more that you can critically reflect on the approach and data, the more it will enable deeper understandings to emerge. In conjunction with this, the use of multiple perspectives and voices will enable a cycle of 'wise practice' (Goodman (2001) cited in Pascal and Bertram, 2012b) to occur where you are not reporting truths but developing perceptions and reflections of practice. As Jacobson (1998: 126) points out, you are constructing knowledge through finding out about how participants see your topic and exploring different perspectives. In doing this you are not constructing findings that can be generalised but 'carefully demonstrating that conclusions represent one credible explanation'. Reflection underpins your selection, handling and interpretation of the data to provide sufficient objectivity to ensure that your relationship to the setting does not lead to a temptation to only find out what you want to hear. This, once again, leads to robust triangulation not only of methods but approaches, and highlights the importance of Nikki's research activator, or any other person that you choose to discuss your research with as it develops (for further discussion of this see Chapter 3). Dialogue with this person can help ensure that you are keeping within your methodological approach, managing your data objectively and maintaining ethicality.

 What factors would you need to consider in constructing your approach? How does your reading support this?

How does critical thinking and reflection inform your choice of approach?

How to start constructing your approach

Nikki has started by thinking about the purpose of her research and how she wanted to gather data. She was clear that she wanted to endeavour to look through the eyes of her participants to build up a picture of parental engagement. This fits with the research objective in finding how parents could be engaged in shaping the services at the centre. The parents may need to feel empowered to contribute to this agenda and a research design that promotes engagement and empowerment in telling the story with parents' views at the core mirrors this. She has an eye to the consequences of her research which will inform practice at her setting and she sees this as just the starting point to ongoing research on the subject. She recognises that the children's centre agenda is subject to change and the role that work-based inquiry can play in informing and driving new policy and practice.

Nikki goes on to tease out the reasons for her project and to set them within her approach. For example, she selects grounded theory as her research is a small-scale project which uses qualitative data to study human interactions within a particular setting, which is her workplace. These are important considerations as your research will likely be carried out within a relatively short time scale, with a limited budget and in a setting with which you are familiar or have selected for the purpose of doing your research. In view of this, your approach will need to recognise these factors in your design. For example, being a small-scale inquiry may mean that your findings will only be particular to that setting, this does not mean that they will not be relevant to others, as is discussed further in Chapter 8. Although bound within a particular context, your findings may potentially make recommendations to illuminate similar issues in other situations.

At this point, it may be helpful to consider using a grid to compare and contrast approaches and their relation to your inquiry. Table 5.1 is an example of a grid based on Nikki's research design. It includes some approaches Nikki could have also considered. This grid gives a snapshot of each approach and should by no means be taken as a definition or considered for your own work without further reading and discussion with tutors and critical friends. No single approach is 'better' than any other and approaches can be combined, as Nikki has done, to make up a personalised and unique approach to an inquiry. Just remember that your chosen approach needs to be supported by relevant sources and explained clearly.

Another approach that Nikki could have considered is praxeological research, because her work-based inquiry embraces a number of key features which Pascal et al. (2012) identify as comprising this method-ology. Praxeology is grounded in real-world situations and acknowledges the unpredictability of human beings and their interactions. It is carried out by practitioners as insiders within a context that will have an immediate use for the results of their work; it is done with people not to people and always in the company of others. It requires the systematic gathering of evidence in order to achieve credibility. It fits with action research in that it is likely to generate theories of action to reveal the underlying motivations, in effect to discover why we do what we do. Pascal argues that the methodology is underpinned by a strong

Table 5.1 Comparing approaches to research

Approach	Key elements	Nikki's research	Sources to consider
Ethnography – giving participants a voice	In-depth study of people in their everyday lives over a period of time Focus on a specific setting Capturing detail within setting Gaining insights in practice See the world through the perspective of those involved in the research – developing relationships	Being a member of a setting In depth over a period of 6 months Using parents with whom she had a relationship and seeing the Stay and Play through their eyes	James (2007)
Grounded research	Small scale, in settings, quantitative data, exploratory. It is based on grounded theory where the data leads the development of theory	Takes place in children's centre. Exploring views using quantitative data	Glaser and Strauss (1987) Glaser (1992)
Action research	Real world, illuminating, exploring change, practical, focus on change and improving practice, feedback, practitioner's role crucial. Need to be able to spend a period of time in the setting. Operates on cycles of reflection on practice	Focus on improving the way parents are engaged in shaping services	McNiff and Whitehead (2010)
Phenomenology	Seeing through the eyes of others, studying the perspectives of others and listening to their voices and using their experience to illuminate or inform	Looking through parents' and practitioners' eyes	Denscombe (2010)
Interpretivist	Detailed insight into an issue. Concerned with how people make sense of the world within a cultural and social framework and shared meanings. Focus on the meaning people ascribe to their experiences and phenomena Small sample in real-world settings Effect of the researcher on the research important – can never be neutral	Detailed insight into parental engagement, through parents' eyes Nikki has not looked at the effect of herself as a researcher, eg an 'insider or outsider' to the research setting	Walsham (2006)
Case study	A detailed investigation of relationships and processes, might be just one facet within the setting Need to set a boundary around the case being studied A snapshot of one point in time	Could apply to Nikki's approach	Stake (1995)
Hermeneutics	Emphasis on learning how to learn: encourages researcher self-direction. The approach is 'fluid' and allows flexibility, self direction and choice; issues are seen from different perspectives and inspires researchers to develop own understandings to make sense of the world	Feedback loop within action research model which depicts the research as a never-ending cyclical process	Hase and Kenyon (2000)

purposeful ethical code and involves critical self-evaluation, reflection and action (praxis); this entails going back again and again throughout the project to rethink and make the work more meaningful. It may result in evidence which transforms views, sheds light and can change practice. All these, I would suggest, are important factors in early years research and can be seen in Nikki's approach.

Nikki could also have considered appreciative enquiry (Cooperrider, 2005) whereby exploration of the positive and successful elements of what works within the research area can lead to reflection on why these work. It can provide opportunities to build on these to see what else could be achieved. Set within a cycle of 'dream', 'design' and 'do' or 'destiny', it incorporates visionary thinking based on what is possible. This approach could have allowed Nikki to see her study in a different light in building on the centre's system of engaging and involving parents in shaping services. This approach particularly lends itself to the prerequisite to work *with* and not *on* settings, in terms of starting from an attitude which looks at what is working at the setting and what can be built upon, rather than intimating that there is a 'problem' which needs sorting out. These two approaches could be added to the grid.

While the grid may seem a simplistic example, it is important to note that there are many sources of literature that discuss different views of each approach and it is important to 'shop around' in deciding your stance. It may, at first glance, seem that many of these approaches are similar and that it is hard to distinguish what would best fit your research aims. The grid gives you a tool to use when comparing and contrasting approaches to see where the emphasis lies in each methodology and which best fits your own ideas and perhaps, where to focus your initial reading.

 Are there other approaches which you have discovered that could be added to the grid?

Catherine's methodology

Catherine explains the rationale for her study in her introduction and introduces a new approach within her methodology as follows:

> The strategy used for this social research into improving services for children in hospital was conducted using a mixed methods approach. The strategy includes the research paradigm and identifies the research problem. Denscombe (2010: 5) states that

all research must clearly demonstrate what it hopes to achieve in order for its purpose to be verified. Evidence from the literature review clearly identifies that the latent conflict between the child's rights and the necessity of fulfilling the assessment criteria of the early year's framework whilst in hospital presents a barrier to learning.

The research strategy that has been employed for this piece of social research is the mixed methods approach. This refers to any strategy that uses both qualitative and quantitative methods and/or deliberately combines a variety of methods from different traditions and with different underlying assumptions (Denscombe, 2010: 137). It has been noted that mixed methods strategies are a relatively new way to examine social phenomena (Gray, 2009: 200). This is because historically researchers have been reluctant to explore the prospects of combining quantitative and qualitative methods on the grounds that they are philosophically irreconcilable (Gray, 2009: 201). To illustrate, quantitative methods are usually depicted as epistemologically objectivist whereas qualitative methods are constructivist.

However, there is a growing consensus that 'treating qualitative and quantitative approaches to research as incompatible opposites is neither helpful nor realistic when it comes to research activity' (Denscombe, 2010: 138). The mixed methods approach not only allows the researcher to analyse evidence from different paradigms but to explicitly focus on the links between the two approaches, otherwise known as 'triangulation'. Laws (2003, cited in Bell, 2005: 116) states that the 'key to triangulation is to see the same thing from different perspectives and thus to be able to confirm or challenge the findings of one method with those of another'. This allows for the researcher to view the phenomenon in a richer and more contextual manner and thus improves the validity of the research.

Indeed, the research problem in question requires an in-depth study and comparison between theory and practice, with the ideal conclusion of improving current practice. Analysis needs to be conducted on systems and policies that are multifaceted, as well as from conflicted disciplines. Therefore the triangulation technique will allow evidence to be compared and drawn together from many spheres of learning.

Commentary

Within her research, Catherine has explored the tensions and contradictions in the rights of the child to engage in play and to have their voice heard, balanced against the lack of autonomy in terms of medical procedures needed and the demands placed upon teachers to deliver and assess the EYFS (DCSF, 2008). Based upon the knowledge gleaned from her literature review she has decided to carry out empirical research (this means collecting data in the physical context, through such tools as observation and interview, as opposed to exploring theory alone) into the conflict between the autonomy of the child versus the pressures of assessments and their status as an active participant in their care. This means that she has selected an approach which has enabled the exploration of theory and practice within the context of social research.

Positioning oneself within your approach is important. The day-to-day interactions and actions that we all take part in influence the bigger picture and determine the culture of organisations and how they work. Studying these helps us to understand how these inform the structure of society and how practice might be improved. Each of us positions ourselves within our daily interactions and ways of being; Tirado and Galvez (2007: 8) describe positioning as 'somewhat like the fine threads that weave the lattice of social interaction'. Positioning comes about through the interactions we make and the stories or episodes that come from this interaction. This makes a map where all the elements of the situation weave together to form a whole which can allow us to gain understanding about how society is managed and how rights and responsibilities, which are central to Catherine's study, evolve. From this, past actions can be identified and made sense of and future practice can be determined.

Fundamental to research with people is the role of the researcher as listener. Stern (2011) asserts that the responsibility of taking on that role involves withholding judgement and to not only listen but to value what is being said. Through the listener pulling together the elements of the research further understandings can emerge. This is why it is so important for your research position to be articulated, so, as Catherine tells us, the richness of the data from conflicting viewpoints can be triangulated and your research position itself can reinforce the robustness of your research. Crotty (1998) in his book *The Foundations of Social Research: Meaning and Perspective in the Research* suggests four elements in choosing an approach which are: theoretical framework (how we know what we know); literature methodology (your approach); and methods which he advocates should be addressed in chronological order as one informs the other. However, these could equally well be integrated to form a holistic approach more suitable to developing early years thinking. By explaining what we mean by these in terms of our research our approach can be built on solid foundations. We can look at these in the light of Catherine's research (see Figure 5.1).

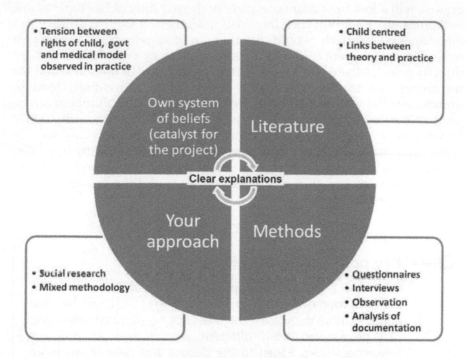

Figure 5.1 Developing an approach

Figure 5.1 shows the four elements of the research design within the circle's quadrants and adjacent to these sit the related aspects of Catherine's research. The model acts rather like a kaleidoscope where the four quadrants can be moved around to assess the quality of the research design in order to ensure that they all fit together to achieve the holistic picture Catherine is looking for. Using this model to help design your research will enable you to see the whole picture of your research underpinned by ethics, as discussed in Chapter 3.

 How can the model (Figure 5.1) illuminate your research in order to present a holistic approach which triangulates your work?

Are there other models you could use, for example, mind mapping?

Catherine has introduced us to an approach which she terms 'mixed methods' whereby data from both qualitative and quantitative data can be used in the same piece of work-based inquiry. This approach is very similar to the case study approach which allows a full range of data collection methods to be used. The mixed methods approach, Catherine argues, will allow for a more complete understanding of her topic as one will build on or support the other. Within Catherine's study using only a quantitative approach would devalue understanding the context or setting in which people practise, as the voices of participants are not directly heard. Mixed methods research is 'practical' in the sense that the researcher can use both methods and because individuals tend to understand the world using both numbers and words. Numbers can be used to represent the bigger picture of the what, whereas individuals' views can give us the detail of the why. This approach, as seen in Catherine's study, can lend itself to complex situations and can appeal to a diverse readership. Catherine argues that using both methods will lead to being able to see different perspectives and thus triangulate the evidence more thoroughly.

 Key points from the chapter

There are a number of approaches that can be adopted to develop your own research methodology. Each can be read about in more detail from the reference list supplied below and can be viewed from different perspectives as different researchers have added to the debate and have learnt more about the varying approaches through their research. New types of approach can come to the forefront through this process and it is useful to find out about these through looking at journals relating to research methods and relevant websites. It is important not to become too confused by the number and types of approach and to select from these to formulate a personal design which fits best with what you are trying to find out, your deeply held values and principles, and how you wish to go about doing your inquiry. This, as we have seen from Nikki's study, can be fluid and may change with new information, and your initial ideas may need renegotiation.

In deciding which approach to use, the models used in Table 5.1 and Figure 5.1 are useful tools to try out in ensuring a holistic approach and in selecting the most important aspects of your approach. However, what is of most importance in designing and writing your project is that you, like Nikki and Catherine, consider a range of approaches and articulate your thought process on why you have chosen or not chosen these for your final selection. How you decide this has implications for potential changes in practice resulting from your findings as, ultimately, it is our responsibility to ensure that our work with children and their families is as sound as possible to ensure the very best outcomes.

Further reading

Denscombe, M. (2010) *The Good Research Guide: For Small Scale Social Research Projects.* 4th edn. Buckingham: Open University Press.

This is a practical guide, taking the researcher from the design of a small-scale research project to the writing up of research findings. It contains useful checklists.

Denzin, N.K. and Lincoln, Y. (eds) (2003) *The Landscape of Qualitative Research: Theories and Issues.* 2nd edn. London: Sage.

This book gives an overview of qualitative research and discusses the importance of triangulation.

McNiff, J. and Whitehead, J. (2011) *All You Need to Know about Action Research.* 2nd edn. London: Sage.

This is an accessible text which gives an insight into action research in practice. It gives clear and straightforward guidance to practitioners.

6 Gathering data

This chapter will:
- Help you to consider whose voices it is most important for you to hear from to tell the story of your research;
- Focus on qualitative data collection;
- Discuss the many choices to be made in collecting data;
- Consider how to avoid some of the common pitfalls in gathering data.

Investigating a small population with care and empathetic concern for participants is rich in potential for detailed analysis using words and images, seeing the world through the eyes of others. There are two main types of data collection: quantitative, which comprises mainly numerical data; and qualitative, which mainly comprises words. Coolican (1990: 49) explains it this way:

> 'Quantification' means to measure on some numerical basis ... Whenever we count or categorise we quantify ... A qualitative approach, by contrast, emphasises meanings, experiences ... descriptions and so on. Raw data will be exactly what people have said ... or a description of what has been observed.

As we have discussed in Chapter 1, early childhood research particularly lends itself to collecting qualitative data in that constructivist and interpretivist paradigms are often used. In view of this, the main focus is on collecting qualitative data in this chapter.

Methods are the tools which enable you to carry out the research. To go back to the building a house analogy discussed in Chapter 5, you need to explain, for example, why you need a cement mixer to lay the foundations. You need to consider suitability for the task. To begin looking at this, Nikki's study (which formed the first part of Chapter 5) has provided a detailed explanation of the decisions she needed to consider prior to deciding upon her data collection methods. She writes:

> Within the investigation I was aware of potential constraints that might need addressing. The primary concern related to the decisions made by individuals. Firstly, would the research be given permission and secondly would people participate? As soon as the research proposal was given permission to proceed by the University, the next step was to seek permission from the RA (Research Activator). The RA was prompt to grant permission and did not impose restrictions that would not allow the research to evolve. Next, co-operation was required by potential participants. I was pleased that I did not face any objections during the course of the research. Furthermore, once the questionnaires were analysed, because of the open communication with the RA, we were able to meet again to reassess the direction of where the research might potentially lead to. Next, I needed to understand how confidentiality might be a constraint so I was explicit how I addressed this matter and considered ethical matters too. Finally, time was to prove the biggest constraint to my research. Completing the study over two semesters initially gave me the idea that I would be under less pressure. However, the reality was that ten months was not a long time and time management was crucial. As a full time student I had essays to complete for other modules, I worked part time; I have three young children and a home to run. Therefore my first step was to devise a time plan. I needed to ensure I had a work, research and home life balance and I was always mindful of how valuable time was. To illustrate this point Rodd (2009, p. 92) states that time management is essentially 'setting goals in one's personal and professional life, and establishing priorities for the tasks to be undertaken in order to achieve these goals'.

Commentary

What is important about Nikki's approach is that she explains her journey and thought processes at every stage of her consideration of data gathering. She discusses her personal constraints of being a busy parent, working and studying and having limited time. It is important to acknowledge that time is likely to be a factor and accept that your research design may not be perfect but that you are striving to look at what is most important for you and worth investigating from the myriad of approaches and information on the topic.

Nikki then discusses the way she intends to go about using her selected methods. This is likely to be individual to your needs within your research question, the resources you and the setting have and your ethical considerations. It is important to enable the reader to understand how you came to decisions and obtained your results. Again, reflecting on these both before and after you collect the data will add to the reliability and validity of your research. It is important to be explicit, for example, about how many observations you did, when you did them, why you chose the participants you observed, the context of the observations, how long they were, how you ensured ethicality and, above all, why you made these decisions.

Nikki goes on to explain her choice of data collection methods:

> The first method of data collection selected was questionnaires. The advantages to this method were they would allow anonymity, be non-partisan and were economical (Denscombe, 2007). Potential disadvantages were; the possibility of unreturned questionnaires; questions could be insufficiently answered or missed out. Additionally I would not have the opportunity to follow up on key issues or check on the truthfulness of answers of the participants (Denscombe, 2007). In an attempt to address the matter of unreturned questionnaires I handed out the questionnaires to participants with a pen and asked if they were able to complete it whilst at the [Children's Centre]. I was aware this could have had ethical issues, yet the parents could have refused, interestingly none did. In fact they commented they would prefer to fill it in now as they would forget or wouldn't have the time at home. I also suspected this co-operation was due to the parents knowing me and the fact there was an existing relationship. I believe the responses would have been quite different otherwise. With regards to missed out answers as the participants were anonymous I could not address that matter. However, with the issue of following up on key issues, I was hopeful that the planned mini focus group would provide me with the opportunity to raise and address participants' responses.
>
> Initial ideas regarding the design of the questionnaires were influenced by Robson (1998) who designed a five point model. This model consisted of an introduction, warm-up, and main body of interview, cool off and closure (Robson, 1998, cited by Siraj-Blatchford, 2008). The introduction consisted of a covering letter to potential participants. The letter gave details of

myself, why I am inviting parents to participate, what the research questions were, and the confidentiality and ethics relating to the study. I then had to consider the general structure of the questionnaire. Hence, I looked at the design of the questions in more detail. The initial questions asked some warm up questions which were seeking general information about the parent and child. The design used open and closed questions. Using open ended questions gives participants the opportunity to fully express themselves in their own manner. Whilst closed questions would elicit either a yes or no answer where the 'structure imposed on the respondent's answers provides the researcher with information which is of uniform length and in a form that lends itself nicely to being quantified and compared' (Denscome, 2007, p. 166). Regarding the design of the individual questions I considered the following: use clear and understandable wording that avoids ambiguity; avoid vagueness and jargon; avoid presumptions and avoid leading questions (Denscombe, 2007, Siraj-Blatchford, 2008). The finished questionnaire had just two closed questions but one of these prompted participants to extend their closed answer.

Commentary

Nikki has used an open discourse to talk through the rationale for her choice of questionnaires. She is forthright in explaining the potential pitfalls and how she has adapted the methods in the light of her particular situation. Importantly, she explores the potential impact of her status within the organisation and how her relationship with each person would influence their participation in filling out the questionnaires. Consideration of how you are going to collect the data in practice is relevant to your choice of method. For example, the relationships that are forged with participants are worth considering, as the quality of response to your data collection will largely depend on this. Parents may be wary about giving details about themselves to someone they do not know. You may be in a position of being an insider, as considered in Chapter 3, where you will know the respondents well and need to consider data collection ethically, particularly if you are in a position of authority. In Nikki's case her relationship with the parents helped as she was able to encourage them to complete the questionnaire then and there. It is worth taking some time in building a relationship with your participants before asking for their contribution and in discussing with them ways of gathering the data which will best suit them.

In my experience, unless respondents complete questionnaires at the time you hand them out you rarely get them back and many students have expressed disappointment in the number of questionnaires they have had returned. It is worth thinking about the possibility of encouraging parental engagement. One way that has been successfully used, for example, is through offering a raffle ticket for a small prize, perhaps a small book token to buy books for the setting or their child, to be given when the completed questionnaire is handed in. This has to be carefully considered but there is a difference between bribing someone to do something and providing a small recognition of their input as a thank you.

Demonstrating the credibility of your research, if using a questionnaire, would be enhanced through taking the time to pilot your questions. This means giving your questionnaire to someone as a 'practice run'. This could be carried out with a group of peers, another setting or other professionals, within your learning groups or with a colleague. It is very difficult to get the questions right first time and you can see from piloting that people interpret questions differently or that they may not understand what you are asking. The quality of the information you obtain from questionnaires is dependent on the way you ask the questions. Students often tell me that they are disappointed with the information they have received and realise too late, how vital it is to have a trial of your data collection tools by someone acting the role of research participant.

Nikki goes on to consider interviews and focus groups as further methods of data collection:

The next method of collecting data was to conduct interviews. I decided I would carry out two types, one to one interviews and a mini focus group. These would be useful as they would follow up the questionnaires, yet they can also be a principle method (Swetman, 2004). Like the questionnaires I gave thoughtful consideration to the advantages and disadvantages of using this method. The advantages can be identified as; adaptable (can provide immediate opportunities for the interviewer to follow up answers which can result in a depth of valuable data being sought); minimal equipment required; high response rate; validity (data can be immediately checked for relevancy and accuracy); and finally that interviews can be rewarding (when compared to methods such as questionnaires or observations since having a personal element can be more enjoyable). Conversely the disadvantages were they are; time consuming (preparation of questions, transcribing the interview and then analysing the data); data analysis can be more time consuming (interviews are more difficult to analyse and record due to the unique response of the interviewee); and confidentiality (there may be a lack of willing participants due to the fact it's not anonymous). However, the main disadvantage to interviews is what is known as the 'interviewer effect' (Denscombe, 2007, p. 184). The data is provided by the spoken words of the interviewee on the issues in question, yet the interviewer must realise that the data and the practice carried out by the interviewee may be very different. Swetman (2004, p. 66) states that as an interviewer I would 'only draw out information compatible with your status'. Furthermore the status of the interviewer and interviewee can impact upon the interview in two ways. Firstly with regards to interviewee inhibitions, if the interview is being recorded this may impact upon the interviewee and secondly the issue is subjective and this may involve bias. Therefore throughout the planning for the interviews and the mini focus group I was aware of how my status could impact on the interviews and that barriers could be created. Personal factors involved in this investigation were I was known to the participants, yet in different capacities. I was a work colleague, member of staff and a practitioner at the CC. It was essential I recognised that every participant would have personal values, interests and views and understand how they might impact upon impartiality and fairness. This would further illustrate how unique each interview would be since I had different relationships with each participant but to each one I had a duty to conduct the interview in an ethical, equitable and responsible manner.

Once consideration had been given to the strengths and weaknesses of using interviews I concluded they would be a useful method. I planned to carry out two one to one interviews and an interview in the format of a mini focus group. However I needed to consider the interview style. The three recognised styles are structured, semi-structured or unstructured; structured – the interviewer has a specific set of identical questions they ask each participant which gives the advantage that the responses can be compared. As a first time interviewer Bell (1999) states this would be the most suitable style to adopt; semi-structured – the interviewer has a specific set of questions but has flexibility regarding the order they are asked in, asking supplementary questions and allowing the interviewee to develop their answers; unstructured – the interviewer introduces a

Continues

Continued

topic or theme and hopefully a 'conversation with a purpose' ensues (Walliman and Buckler, 2008, p. 173). This style does allow for a discussion with depth but does require the interviewer to be experienced and more importantly have a lot of time to analyse the data.

Having considered that I am a first time researcher with limited time I decided to use a structured style which would allow me to compare answers. Since the investigation involved examining current practice within the CC I felt it would be useful to consider perspectives from different members of staff. Therefore I asked both interviewees the same questions. Asking the same questions to both interviewees would ensure a degree of standardisation and also mean that analysing the data would be easier (Bell, 1999). Swetman (2004, p. 65) believes that all interviews are a 'structured way of obtaining information on a focused content'. Hence, it was essential I considered that the questions I devised for the interviews were an implement to gaining information from the participants. Furthermore that the questions encouraged them to think, focus and relax when providing answers, to that end it was useful to ask the interviewees how they feel and what their thoughts were (Rudestam and Newton, 2001).

The second style of interview was a mini focus group. Denscombe (2004, p. 178) believes focus groups have three distinctive features; 'focus, interaction within the group [and the ability to] facilitate'. Firstly, the focus in this investigation would be the original questionnaires that the potential participants took part in. Secondly, I would need to have a strong interaction with the participants during the focus group in order that information can be sought. Finally, it was essential I not only facilitated interaction within the group, but also ensured the discussion is specific. A focus group would provide participants with the opportunity to share and compare their views. These views can 'lead in either of two directions – both of which can be of value to the researcher' (Denscombe, 2007, p. 179). The first route is that the group mostly concur with each other and demonstrate a shared viewpoint. The second route is the group clearly exposes differences in their viewpoint. The selection of potential participants invited to join the focus group would inevitably be affected by certain practical factors; potential participants should be able to attend; should be willing to attend at a specified time and date and be willing to give up a few hours of their time; they needed to be relevant to the research,

Points for selection of focus group participants

in this case, the participants had to have taken part in the questionnaires. Whichever the outcome the focus group would certainly provide the research with insight into what the participants thought and possibly why they held that viewpoint (Denscombe, 2007).

Before I started to analyse the data I reflected on the methods of data collection. Overall I was very satisfied with what had been collected and I had stuck within the proposed timescale for gathering the data. In contrast organising and analysing the data took longer than anticipated. I was aware that this would take a considerable amount of time, particularly typing up transcripts, but was not prepared for the actual time involved in the process.

Commentary

Nikki recognises that each person interviewed will have their own voice and opinions and that she must ensure that these are reported impartially. She has considered the potential for researcher bias within her discussion of carrying out interviews and acknowledges the unique relationship she has with each participant. She understands that a degree of self-reflexivity is needed to distinguish and be open about how personal choices and opinions could affect the data. Using a structured interview approach not only supported her as a new researcher but prevented her going off on tangents and asking leading questions.

You may be wondering whether it is really possible to be completely objective or unbiased in being either an insider or an outsider to the research setting. In small-scale social research, is it actually necessary to say you are unbiased? A strong code of ethics, or saying you are adopting standards of good practice, does not always assure the reader that the research is objective. As Carr (2000) argues, you are likely to hold views on what you are researching and as a social scientific researcher you cannot be unbiased. This is discussed more fully in Chapter 7. Jacobson (1998) draws our attention to the practitioner as the 'instrument', through which meanings within the topic are explored, as such 'the collector'cannot be separated from the data collection. He goes on to suggest that the integrity of the research comes from the quality of action as a result of the research findings, that the quality of the data collected, must clearly identify what was actually seen rather than what you want to see. This must include data collected from a variety of sources. The issue of bias should, therefore, not be ignored. Rather, objectivity requires the research to be related to the values you hold as an early years practitioner and these need to be made clear and integral to the inquiry. Just as asking children to make transitions from one setting to another, for example, requires courage on their part, the practitioner making the transition to researcher needs to hold true to a sense of professional identity and values and be courageous in recognising and debating these within the research. Nikki, in the excerpt above, discusses the take-up of her questionnaire and acknowledges that she received the questionnaires back and the response within them largely because of her relationship to the participants. It is this honesty and self-reflection that help to give the research its credibility. Reflecting on your relationships with participants will allow the reader to understand the authenticity of your work.

Nikki puts consideration of her participants at the forefront of her planning within her choice of methods and considers how they might respond, what pitfalls she may encounter, and she has thought through ways around potential difficulties. She also takes into account that she is a first-time researcher and that although, within interviews for example, she would have liked to use a semi-structured or unstructured approach, a consequence of her relative inexperience was that she felt it was likely to gain more accurate results by using structured questions. Her discussion leads the reader to trust Nikki's approach as she demonstrates an understanding of the issues and will be careful to take account of these within her research.

Reflecting back on your design at each stage, as you can see Nikki has in relation to her mini focus groups, will enable you to keep a continuous check on the appropriateness of your methods in relation to your question and your approach. This will demonstrate to the reader that you have been rigorous and reliable in your research and exude a greater level of confidence in the gathered data.

 Keeping a research diary of the day-to-day interactions that occur in relation to your research is a good way to capture data. It is surprising how once you start researching, the topic comes up frequently during the course of the day or perhaps you are more attuned to these sorts of discussions taking place. Capturing these at the time, gives you a wealth of information and source of quotes on which to draw in your writing. Do not forget to include the date and context in which it was gathered in order to authenticate the data and, more importantly, remember to seek permission before presenting others' views within your study.

Nikki considers how she intends to ensure the reliability and validity of her work. She writes:

Measuring validity and reliability within research is an essential yet complex job. According to Walliman and Buckler (2008, p. 207):

'Validity refers to the accuracy of a result, whether the collected data is representative and illustrates the phenomenon. As such its level of trueness. Reliability refers to the consistency of the data: if the same data collection methods were used with a similar sample, would similar results be obtained?'

Ensuring the data was valid and reliable was crucial. I was undertaking an interpretivist approach and MacNaughton et al. (2001, p. 36) acknowledge for 'interpretivists, knowledge is valid if it is authentic, that is the true voice of the participants in their research'. To demonstrate the authenticity of participants' answers I chose to use triangulation, using triangulation meant that the data could be corroborated between methods. Using a range of methods in the research meant I could compare and combine the findings to gain a better insight into my topic (Cohen, Manion and Morrison, 2000 cited in Roberts-Holmes, 2005). This method is known as methodological triangulation and it uses 'multiple methods to study a single problem' (MacNaughton et al., 2008, p.124). I realised this approach would not only give different perspectives but also demonstrate corroboration within the findings which consequently aid validity (Denscombe, 2007). As my primary aim was to seek qualitative data I decided that the best method for achieving this was to use questionnaires and interviews.

Commentary

Nikki wanted her research to be seen as credible and to make a real contribution to practice at her setting. She therefore needed her research to ring true and to be believed in by her audience. She first turns to the concepts of validity and reliability to help her with this.

The essence of reliability and validity is the trustworthiness of your research, which relates to your professional responsibilities to children and families. In order to gain the most accurate information you may consider talking to the people who know best about the subject under research. This will influence your choice of data collection methods. It may not necessarily mean that you will have a large sample of people to talk to but the people you do consult with will be the experts in the particular question you are asking, as it may relate to their life as parents or children or their professional practice. When talking to children and parents as part of your role as an early years practitioner, you may be empowering them to find their voice. This is why you should listen very carefully to them and report what they say with accuracy. You should be open and honest with them and do what you say you are going to do. This is the same as with your research as a whole, using these principles will allow you to demonstrate reliability and validity within your approach.

While considering your choice of methods it is essential to return to your research question and to ask yourself if your methods are the most appropriate way to find out what you want to know, as Denscombe (2010) advocates, asking yourself if the methods selected are suitable, feasible and ethical. The model in Table 6.1 is a way in which you may see at a glance how Nikki's methods work together to form a holistic picture of data collection to inform her question.

Table 6.1 Triangulating methodology and data

Research method	What data will this provide?	Notes
Questionnaire	Initial survey of views, provides an overview	
Interview	Direct answers for specific questions arising from questionnaire	
Literature review	Provides a formal line of inquiry as a starting point	
Mini focus group	Creating a community of research practice, face-to-face interaction. Opportunities for new ideas to be developed through discussion	

As you can see Nikki completes her discussion of reliability and validity by explaining how these have informed her choice of methods.

Chapter 1 gives four questions to consider when devising a research question. It is useful to return to these when considering which data collection methods to use.

- Are they **ethical**? Or is there any possibility of them invading privacy or causing offence?

- Are they **purposeful** in that they will improve your understanding or your practice?

- Are they **specific and focused** enough for a small-scale project?

- Can the question that you have formulated **actually be answered** by using these methods?

A common pitfall here is in ensuring that the methods are fit for purpose not only when choosing the method, but also when putting it into practice. For example, if Nikki sets out to interview an early years practitioner about the effectiveness of communication in shaping services for children and families and is instead given information on the practitioner's qualifications and how she manages sessions with children and parents, the interview will not provide the information required and, as such, will not be fit for purpose.

Triangulation

Nikki considers the importance of triangulation which she deems as central to the success of her project. Using more than one method, as Nikki has done, will give the opportunity to show that your evidence is corroborated and more likely to be valid. Planning out your methods as a whole will provide a framework demonstrating the veracity of your research. There are several different ways of going about this. For example, you can triangulate your methods with the approach you are taking to show a rigour in your design. If we take the example of a praxeological approach as demonstrated in Table 6.2, according to Pascal and Bertram (2012) this is underpinned by the following principles: subjective in that it acknowledges multiple perspectives, systematic, action based, educational, democratic in the sense of being inclusionary, participatory and collaborative, ethical, empowering, dynamic, critical in the sense of being risky, and requiring courage and political in being concerned with social justice and equity. If we consider some common methods used in the light of this, areas of crossover can be seen. This table provides a clearly triangulated plan you can see at a glance whether the methods are fit for purpose and provide a robust framework from which to begin the research.

Undertaking such an exercise with your own approach and choice of methods can enable you to see how these fit together to form a triangulated framework from which to carry out your research.

It is not the purpose of this chapter to discuss the practical aspects and considerations within each possible research method as there are many good books listed at the end of the chapter which give sound advice on this. However, there are some pitfalls which students often come across in choosing and gathering data, some of which I discuss below.

Observations

Although observations afford the researcher valuable insights into the participant's world, they are not an easy method of collecting data. They need to be carefully considered both in terms of ethics and structure. Consideration of ethics, particularly in relation to observing children, can be found in Chapter 3. However, it is worth thinking about the structure

Table 6.2 Holistic view of triangulation

Methods	Praxeology approach	Objectives	Data
Questionnaires Open questions Closed questions Scales Multiple choice	Ethical Purposeful Systematic	How the children's centre works in partnership with parents	Initial survey of views, provides an overview
Interviews Structured Semi structured	Ethical Empowering Educational	How parents are included in shaping services at the children's centre	Direct answers for specific questions arising from questionnaire
Focus group Structured Semi structured	Ethical Subjective Dynamic Critical Democratic Acknowledges multiple perspectives Risky and courageous Inclusionary, participatory, collaborative	How parents can be involved in improving individual services at the centre	Creating a community of research practice, face-to-face interaction
Documentary analysis (this could have been used in Nikki's study)	Purposeful Systematic Critical	What were the stated aims of the children's centre in involving parents?	Provide a comparison of policy and practice

of observations when choosing your methods. First, identifying what you think might be gained from doing an observation must be at the centre of your research construction. Ask yourself if the advantages outweigh the potential ethical issues that this would involve. Then think through whom you will observe, at what point in the day, for how long, how you will choose the children/professionals/parents. What type of observation will you be using? Papatheodorou et al. (2011), for example, discuss the role that the researcher takes during observations through a series of vignettes. Will the researcher, for example, be part of the observation or will they remain non-participant? How will they respond to queries from the children or the children requesting their attention or help? However, for observations to have a richness of data the researcher needs to take account of the relationship and shared experience between the setting, the observed and observers. Observations gain far more value when they are clearly contextualised.

It is important to think closely about what you are looking for and the best way of recording this. What will you actually be writing down? For example, in Harriet's study where she looked at this issue of how cultural diversity is supported at a setting within the home corner, she explained her reasoning behind using this method, the way in which she set up the observation, what she would be observing and why, the impact of her location as an observer and the need for multiple observations to provide a meaningful insight. She writes:

Observation is suitable as an initial research method for this study. This is because it is an effective means to provide foundations for the project since it allows a basis for the 'context' of the investigation and produces 'deep, rich data'; a particular focus as a predominantly qualitative researcher (Burton et al., 2008: 97). Additionally, Foster (2006) contends that observation is an efficient way to make certain that data collected via alternative methods is supported. In this way, by asking a child about how they play with peers in the role-play area and observing the child in action; there is greater chance of identifying the truth of the child's statement by identifying whether both methods complement each other.

The intention for this research is to observe children playing together in the 'home-corner' role-play area of the focus setting to reveal any information that might indicate how this play affects their social potential. As the 'home corner' is a freely chosen activity, there is no specific sample of children to be observed and as a researcher; use will be made of observing the children that choose to play in the area. This is an ideal approach from an interpretive outlook, being that the focus is to observe several individuals during social play to create a perception of the various voices and actions of different people (Burton and Bartlett, 2009). As a researcher, there is flexibility over the concept of participant observation where I may become involved in the observations themselves (Bell, 2010) due to possible invitations from children of the research sample to become involved in their play. Tinson (2009) advocates this method of researching with children by stating that it is: 'a useful way in which to build trust and rapport' with them yet it is also important to identify the opinions of Aubrey et al. (2000) in that being accepted in the 'child group' as an adult presents a challenge.

Consequently, the main intention as an observer is to create 'narrative reports' of action in the 'home corner' area of the

Continues

Continued

setting to record all observable details of child participants' 'narrative reports' of action in the 'home corner' area of the setting including verbal exchanges, physical activities and body language to demonstrate the atmosphere of the environment (Woods, 2005: 11). Hobart and Frankel refer to this form of observation as a 'written record' and explain its suitability 'to record a naturally occurring event' such as the action in the 'home corner' area. However, Foster (2006) indicates that child participants might alter their performance due to an awareness of the observer; producing false depictions of role-play events and therefore invalidates results. In this respect, observing at a location away from the direct action may avoid this issue.

In terms of biased data, Hobart and Frankel (2004: 8) emphasise that the researcher has a responsibility through observation to be 'entirely objective' and so record data honestly in a 'detached and impartial manner,' taking note only of what is seen and heard. It is also important to ensure that when observing children from diverse cultural backgrounds as is necessary in this study, there is an appreciation that practices may vary between cultures and so children may be expected to act differently (Hobart and Frankel, 2004). Familiarity of the setting, staff and children alike and the opportunities to talk to practitioners about cultural variation amongst children will be inevitably beneficial. Hobart and Frankel (2004) further suggest that good research requires multiple observations to devise conclusions, given that limited data will not achieve a real insight into the issues observed, hence the aim to record on several opportunities.

In this example, you can identify how Harriet has thought through her role as an adult within the observation and some of the challenges she may encounter in carrying this out. She has highlighted the need for a flexible approach and the importance of building trusting relationships with the children. This is highlighted in Chapter 3 (within the discussion of ethics in relation to researching with children). Harriet has also decided exactly what data she will be recording and how.

Significant sample?

This leads to the issue frequently debated by students as to what constitutes 'enough' data. This will vary according to each study but it is important to explain and to reflect at each stage of data collection on the impact of the amount of data collected in relation to the scope of your project. Could the views that you have collected be considered as significant enough to represent the 'group'? You will have to use a common-sense approach to this and not make claims that are beyond the limits of your data.

 Key points from the chapter

- Explain your thought processes at each stage of devising data collection methods.

- Ensure that you provide the context of your methods clearly, for example, how many children this involved, how many observations and when.

- Taking time to build trusting relationships with participants is crucial to the success of your data collection.

- Honesty and self-reflection within your written submission enables the credibility of your research.

- Listen carefully to your participants and ensure their voices shine through.

- Plan how your methods will support triangulation of your data.

Further reading

Callan, S. and Reed, M. (eds) (2011) *Work-Based Research in the Early Years*. London: Sage.
This book gives clear advice on the building blocks for investigating practice and the selection of meaningful methods for your study.

Denscombe, M. (2010) *The Good Research Guide: For Small-Scale Social Research Projects*. 4th edn. Buckingham: Open University Press.
This book provides an accessible introduction and overview of research methods.

Papatheodorou, T., Luff, P. and Gill, J. (2011) *Child Observation for Learning and Research*. Harlow: Pearson.
This clear and readable text gives advice on organising and carrying out observations with children.

7 Data analysis

Analysing data is a daunting prospect and tends to strike fear into many students. In this chapter we explore:

- The conundrum of analysing qualitative data;
- How issues such as reliability and validity sit within such a personal process;
- Some simple approaches that can make data analysis more manageable;
- Approaches to presenting your results.

What type of data?

In this chapter we are going to focus upon qualitative data, not because there is no worth in quantitative data, on the contrary, discovering that 90 per cent of parents are unhappy about something is a very significant piece of information to hold. The reason that we are focusing on qualitative data is because the majority of practitioner research results in this and it is extremely tricky to know where to start with it. Quantitative data, in comparison, is quite straightforward, and if you would like some very practical support with this area then a good starting point would be Bell (1993); when dealing with quantities, she offers 20 pages of very clear and accessible advice on analysing any numbers (quantitative data) that you collect.

There are a number of methods that you can use to present data, and several of these have been included in this book: grids or tables which are useful for comparison, charts, graphs of all kinds, weaves, patchwork presentations and many more. You need to consider very carefully the data that you have to hand and how that could be most effectively presented. With qualitative data especially you should 'play' with it. Some students feel that all research studies should include a graph of some kind. This is certainly not the case and, when dealing with small numbers in particular, it can look a little silly. It makes more sense to discuss that '90 per cent of parents felt that ...' than to include a graph showing that nine parents thought one thing and one parent thought another. You must carefully consider fitness for purpose and appropriateness.

Are your results valid?

It is important to consider the validity and the reliability of your data, although these notions are somewhat restricted within very small-scale research. Although we have touched upon this when discussing data collection methods in Chapter 6, we briefly visit it again within the context of data analysis. Reliability, to some extent, alludes to the consistency with which you have carried out your data collection and your consideration of effecting factors. For example, if you were exploring different approaches to an activity and how engaged the children were, a number of things would have to remain consistent: the children involved, the environment (that is, how distracting the rest of the area is), the time of day that the activity was carried out, what has gone before and the duration of the activity. Of course, there are numerous other variables when dealing with human participants and you can only 'control' some. If any of the factors above were changed between activities, then you would no longer be able to compare like with like. In the same way, if questions that were given to individuals were worded differently, then you would not be able to compare the answers. The 'stability of the measurements' (Mukherji and Albon, 2010: 193) is central to reliability.

Validity deals with how effectively the data you have collected proves the point that you are making. For example, you could not take an informal conversation with two parents as 'proof' that a school of 230 pupils has an effective parent–school partnership. The data does not 'sustain' the claim (Cohen et al., 2001: 107). In order to validate claims you need to have collated as convincing a range of proof as possible. This might include samples of parents' views from all classes via interview or questionnaire (based upon set questions that can then be compared), the views of the teachers, the school policy and a range of other documentary evidence and observations of parent-focused activities. By collating a range of evidence, claims made in one piece of evidence can then be compared to the claims made in another, the evidence can be **triangulated**. In his exploration of ethnography Fetterman (2010: 94) describes triangulation this way: 'compar[ing] information sources to test the quality of the information (and the person sharing it), to understand more completely the part that the actor plays in the social drama, and ultimately to put the whole situation into perspective'. For example, are the claims made in a policy enacted in day-to-day practice? Do the views of parents on a specific topic correspond to those of practitioners? By the time you have compared all of your evidence you should be clear whether you are in a position to make a valid claim or not. You may even find yourself with completely conflicting pieces of information and be in a position where you need to either find an additional, verifying piece of data, or explore more fully during your discussion the reasons for the dichotomous views. Hammersley and Atkinson (1983: 199) warn us not be overly 'optimistic' and assume that 'the aggregation of data from different sources will unproblematically add up to produce a more complete picture' as this is not always the case.

 Have you already come across contradictory data when beginning the analysis of your results? If you are still collecting data, then you could think about further data that may confirm these findings for you. If this is not possible (or you choose not to) then it is good to reflect upon why different views might be held and represented. What has influenced these views?

Notions of validity and reliability take on a more flexible nature when dealing with predominantly qualitative data. As Barab and Squire (2004: 10) explain, 'if a researcher is intimately involved in the conceptualisation, design, development, implementation, and researching of a pedagogical approach, then ensuring that researchers can make credible and trustworthy assertions is a challenge'. And clearly it is, but then there is no aspect of research that is not a challenge. We discussed how approaches to the research should be made transparent in Chapter 2 as preconceptions are likely to influence conclusions. And it is the same with insider knowledge when collecting and analysing data, but rather than this being a negative thing, Anderson and Shattuck (2012: 18) comment that 'inside knowledge adds as much as it detracts from the research validity'. Being a part of a situation can bring a depth of understanding to the data that an outsider could never achieve. In any type of research which involves a deeper exploration of processes, meanings and understanding, although statistical analysis might be used initially to discover overall trends, there will inevitably be an element of the researcher making their own judgements on qualitative data. It is important to be careful to look back to your original questions and seek out answers within your data, rather than succumbing to the temptation of using fortuitous results produced by your data to prove additional (and not necessarily related or useful) points.

As Anderson and Shattuck (2012) discuss in their exploration of design-based research (an approach to research which is situated within a real educational context with the aim of informing and improving practice), we would expect all of our practitioners to share an emotional attachment with the setting in which they are carrying out their research. We would expect them to be an active player within that research context. If not, then they are not fulfilling their role as an early years practitioner. Because of this, analysis becomes more difficult than in an experimental, detached approach, and 'a certain wisdom is needed to walk the line between objectivity and bias' (Anderson and Shattuck, 2012: 18).

There is no answer to this, and rather than attempting to 'solve' it, it should be embraced within the research. The researcher is not setting out on the research with a 'clean slate', but instead, what Luca (2009: 22) refers to as:

> 'embodied bracketing' ... involves researchers feeling comfortable to bring into their investigation pre-existing knowledge and experience, allowing ourselves to affectively engage with the research, whilst recognising and making transparent the possible impact we may have on the research. Embodied bracketing for me means placing my assumptions and preconceptions in parenthesis. This way they are constantly accessible for reflection. It is here that researchers embodied subjectivities could be seen as the 'gloss' of the entire process. The idea of 'embodied bracketing' is about wholeness and integrity of understanding.

Luca (2009: 22) believes that in the meeting of two sets of knowledge (participant and researcher) 'understanding becomes illuminated'.

So where do we begin? With any qualitative research the first step is to submerge oneself in the data collected. What follows are some very basic steps towards effective qualitative data analysis.

 Submergence in data. Read and reread your data as a whole until it is familiar to you. This will help you to find your way around it when you begin analysis. As you read and reread you will notice particular themes or key points begin to emerge; make a note of these. Sometimes these will be ideas that you were not expecting to see, but prove to be significant. I always say to my students that if they were telling someone else about their research and had to tell them three to five key findings that they discovered through their data, what would these be? What has stood out in your data?

The first step, above, is something that is often overlooked, by students and theorists alike, as it is taken for granted. Roberts-Holmes (2011) goes straight into reducing data (which I will discuss shortly) and you will notice that both excerpts from students skip immediately to key themes. When discussing your 'research journey' do be sure to include how you first approached your data. Norton (2009), uses a similar term, which is 'immersion' in the data, and it is important that you consider the data as a whole instead of immediately focusing upon key ideas or key questions. Mukherji and Albon (2010: 230) refer to it as '*Becoming familiar with the data*'. This will give you an idea of the concepts that keep re-emerging, which may well be quite different to the 'answers' that you were expecting. It may also illuminate for you the views that you expected to find which are missing from your data. It is important to consider your data as a whole entity and avoid the temptation to focus only on the answers that you were seeking. When you have thoroughly engaged with your data as a whole, step back from it and consider the key concepts that have emerged.

Next comes **data reduction**, which Emily (below) refers to as 'filtering'. It is referred to in many ways, 'coding', 'categorising', 'tabulating', but it basically involves identifying segments of text as belonging to various categories. This can be done by highlighting the text in different colours, giving codes to different phrases or literally cutting and pasting the text into a table. The example in Table 7.1 looks at how a grid was used to begin to organise and analyse data that looked at approaches to behaviour management in two reception classes. This small section from the data categorisation shows how you can begin to see similarities and differences between the data, aligned to multiple perspectives of the same phenomenon.

Whichever way you go about data organisation, categorisation, or filtration as Emily referred to it, it ultimately involves recognising and drawing together all of the data that refers to a particular theme. I hope that you can recognise at this point that this is a completely different process to going through each data collection method and presenting all of the answers to each question. By coding, all of your different pieces of data are compared, triangulated and, eventually, assimilated.

As you will remember from the introduction, Emily explored how policy change impacted upon a children's centre. Her data predominantly comprised of observations (in the form of journal entries) and formal and informal interview records. When Emily categorised her collated data, three key themes emerged:

• Tension;

• Interprofessional working;

• Meeting needs.

Emily explores these themes using both qualitative and quantitative data analysis. Radnor (2002: 90) comments that it is only after that initial analysis that you really begin to interpret your results: 'This is

Table 7.1 Organising and analysing data

Theme	Teacher interview	Parent questionnaire	School behaviour policy	Displays in class
Positive encouragement	'Sometimes just a smile is enough for children to double their efforts' TR1 'I always give a secret wink to children that I am pleased with. That shows a secret understanding between the two of us that I am really pleased with them without making a big fuss' TR1 'We use a sticker chart when the children have done well. You will see all of the children sit up beautifully when they think that they might get a sticker …' TR2 'Punishment makes no difference at all, only reward. We use the old adage of "catch them being good"' TR2	'I like that my child regularly comes home with a little sticker or certificate to say that she has tried hard. She is certainly not "top of the class" so it is nice that her efforts are recognised in other ways' PR1 'In my son's old school he was regularly punished for bad behaviour and things never seemed to improve. Since he's been in this school there have been no problems at all. They seem to recognise that he is just an active little boy and give him lots of encouragement to try harder. He has his own sticker chart that he brings home' PR2	The school policy states the children will be rewarded for good behaviour and that this will vary from class to class. It encourages teachers to make parents aware of these approaches and, where necessary, to engage regularly with them. It states that the school will work actively with parents if any problems arise.	R1 has a 'star of the week' board. This has various categories such as 'working hard' and being a good friend. R2 has a sticker chart for each child on display. Some children have a large number of stickers and some just a few. It would appear that those with behaviour problems collect more stickers for encouragement. *Follow up: question the teacher about this.*
Reinforcement of parameters	'Whenever there are problems we remind the children of the rules that they wrote with us at the beginning of the year' TR2 'Although I encourage the children as much as I possibly can they also know that they will be punished if they persist. They also know that I will talk with their parents at the end of the day …' TR1	'My child will occasionally mention that a child has been "naughty" but these appear to be one off occasions and managed well. A few parents have been "summonsed" by the teacher, but I've avoided that so far, thank goodness …' PR1	Each class will devise its own 'class rules' at the beginning of the year. These will be clearly displayed and the children will be reminded of the expectations regularly …	R1 has Golden Rules where each of the rules is written as a positive; 'we will speak kindly etc'. R2 has the same as above but has included photos of the children in the class displaying those behaviours. All of the children are included in the photos …

when you go on to explore and seek out relationships and patterns, making connections across topics and categories'.

And this brings us to the third point in the process, **using strong examples to support your analysis**. What has been said, what have you read or what have you observed that exemplifies the point being made most effectively? Which are your 'strongest' pieces of data? These can then be used to support the 'argument' that you will put forward. Here we see just one of Emily's themes explored more fully, using evidence from her observations and interviews to support the points that she makes.

Interprofessional Working

In the background and literature section of this study I have been able to identify how interprofessional working is a very important part of practice within the context of Sure Start Children's Centres. The successful interprofessional working in Sure Start Children's Centres has often been ascribed to the co-location nature of the centres, where a broad range of professionals from the different sectors of Health, Education, Early Years and Social Care work alongside each other under one roof. In my research I interviewed 63% of the regular team of Children Centre staff about their understanding of interprofessional working. A list of 26 named professionals was provided in a checklist, based upon the different professionals I had encountered. This was certainly not a comprehensive list of all professionals who are involved in the centre as it was based upon my own experiences: although opportunity was provided for interviewees to add other professionals which were not included on the list. An additional 13 professionals were identified during the course of the interviews (Appendix 4). It could also be argued that many more professionals may have been identified if the staff members had been given opportunity to reflect upon their experiences. Unfortunately, due to the time constraints it was not possible to plan opportunity for a preview of the interview.

It was important for me to identify out of the named list of professionals how many of them the team of staff had encountered. I also needed to distinguish if staff members had or had not benefited from being co-located and if they perceived that professionals were made more accessible to themselves and the parents with whom they worked as a result.

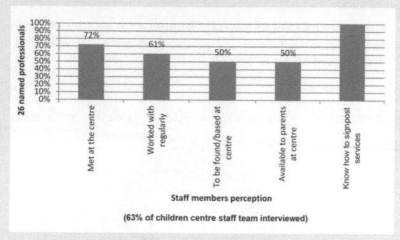

7.1 Children's centre staff understanding of integrated working

It is interesting to identify that out of the staff interviewed they were only able to identify 61% of the professionals listed as having worked with them. This perhaps reflects the different roles carried out by team members, for example a family support worker may have a better knowledge base of interprofessional working than a centre worker. A thought provoking statement made by a senior member of staff who demonstrated an extensive knowledge of a wide range of professionals at the centre, indicated that pressures placed on their own roles because of policy change such as file audits and hot-desking had impacted upon team members' ability to be aware of the wider context;

'To cope with the changes and my role I have had to ask myself do I really need to know everything about the centre and know who is there, for example if the Health Visitors are in or what's on? But hot-desking has had an impact because – who is in? Who is at my seat? – it is just too difficult so you have to focus on your own role or it becomes too much.'

It was possible to explore individuals' roles in more detail, for example one question asked the interviewees which sector they describe themselves as working in: Education, The Early Years Sector, Health or Social Care. The promotion of interprofessional working and co-locations has been described as aiming for unity across these sectors, moving away from previous professional barriers between the sectors involved in supporting children. My analysis of the data reflects this. Diagram 7.3 demonstrates

Continues

Continued

a fairly even spread of opinion favouring only slightly the Early Years Sector. In fact, many of the staff team described that they worked across all sectors.

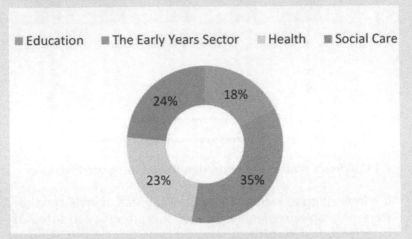

Figure 7.2 Staff members' perception of roles

The attitude of the staff team towards co-location was very positive with 100% of interviewees providing positive results, for example;

'Yes – it leads to better communication; it leads to a better understanding of each other's role. I think it leads to more respect of each other's role, it leads to being able to zone in on specialist skills very quickly and I think you get more quality back from them because you know them and they know you, it leads to … just better working together – yeah its fab actually having people under one roof.'

The centre manager's view of co-location below, displays her commitment and passion for best practice, which appears to have been transferred to the staff members. Indeed, this enthusiastic attitude was present in all of the answers, which reflected a tremendously positive team attitude.

'Definitely! Absolutely definitely! Because it is about using peoples skill base to the best, the BEST use. So that expertise, … you know how you can link in or gain information from, or sign post families to. And also being co- located means that a lot of duplication in what people are offering is hugely reduced so actually you are much more cost effective.'

Indeed, the interview sample showed staff members felt confident about signposting 100% of the named professionals. It was highlighted by another staff member who identified that interprofessional working was working well in this centre and attributed that cohesiveness to the team leadership;

'Here it is working well, we have a team of regular people and good leadership makes a huge difference but in other places (children's centres) I know it is not working so well.'

Commentary

The strength of the discussion that Emily presents is in the voice of her participants being clearly presented. Many students will talk about their data without actually sharing any examples at all. If you have felt that a piece of data is really 'strong', then others are likely to feel that way too, so share it. Construct your data analysis so that your data has the opportunity to 'speak for itself'.

You will notice that Emily's data analysis does not focus upon comparing her findings to literature within this section. Emily only alludes to a few pieces of research very briefly. Whether you bring in references from your original literature search at this stage really is up to you; there are mixed views about it. I tend to encourage students to leave the comparison with literature for a separate, discussion chapter, to allow a focus upon the data by itself. My concern is that discussion will be restricted only to those issues that have already been raised in the literature review and that rich new findings might be overlooked. Haverkamp and Young (2007: 288) disagree with this and comment that, '"Precious comments" made by others need not constrain one's own contributions and conclusions, but the thoughtfulness and utility of the new contribution will be enhanced by understanding what has already been discussed'. Catherine's section, which follows shortly, uses the approach of presenting the data, then analysing it with reference to literature. You do need, at some point, to make reference to literature in order to reflect upon your results, but exactly where this happens is within your control. The three stages (Figure 7.3) can occur separately, with literature not being brought in until stage two or three, or they can be combined. Data can be presented and analysed at the same time, with literature not being referred to until later, in the discussion; or data could be presented, analysed and compared with literature all within one section. It is important that you consider your own data and the approach that will best fit its exploration.

On a number of occasions within her data analysis Emily refers to appendices, and she does this effectively. Appendices can provide additional information that adds a further dimension to a discussion, but the text should still flow freely, and explain the point thoroughly, without the reader *having* to refer to them. If the reader has to repeatedly stop and refer to appendices in order for an argument to make sense, they will soon lose interest.

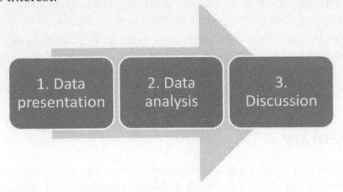

Figure 7.3 Stages of data presentation

Catherine explored how the educational needs of children within a hospital were being met. Although she used a variety of data collection methods (including interview, observation, questionnaire and documentary analysis) she has started by presenting her data in a quantitative way, giving an overview of the results. She then discusses the implications of these results in more detail, using a more qualitative approach. During this discussion she draws in literature that she has reviewed previously. Although she has set this out slightly differently to Emily, she still begins by presenting the key findings to emerge from her investigation. This provides a framework for the discussion that follows.

She writes:

Findings

This chapter displays the findings established from the data collected ... The key findings identified barriers to learning, such as poor environment, both by the bedside and in specific early years areas, further training for play therapists regarding the early years curriculum as well as collaboration between services. Areas of success were most notably activities using the Early Years Foundation Stage (EYFS) and improving the child's autonomy through individual target setting.

The first sets of results considered are the responses from the questionnaires. These represent considered views from the hospital teachers and teaching assistants. Figure 7.4 represents how many times each category was mentioned by percentage. This clearly demonstrates the spread of data and the frequency of categories mentioned, however it did not identify the opinions of each category. Therefore, further coding was done to demonstrate positive and negative views regarding each category.

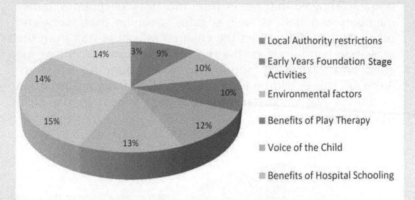

7.4 Coding category frequency by percentage

For example, the category 'Environment' accounted for only one tenth of opinions raised during the initial coding. However, when the categories were broken down into positive and negative views, the impact of the environment of children and professionals teaching in hospital carried the fewest number of positive comments, only 13% and highest number of negative comments, significantly 70%. This was clearly an area that needed to be investigated further. Figure 7.5 illustrates the positive comments coded by percentage and Figure 7.6 illustrates the negative comments coded by percentage.

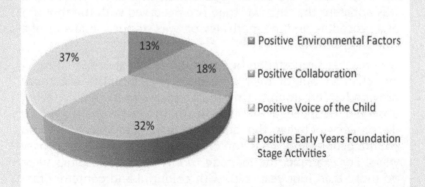

Figure 7.5 Positive comments by coding category

The main concerns about the environment were that it was noisy, cluttered and distracting. In my observations these issues

Continues

Continued

were apparent. Evidence gathered from five wards in two hospitals showed that noises from monitors, telephones, family members and staff as well as drips, cleaning machinery and other children did distract the children as well as staff from the activity in hand. Indeed, the most notable distraction was the cries and distressed sounds from surrounding children. Although some children were unaffected, hearing another child in distress was understandably causing concern to the child having their lesson.

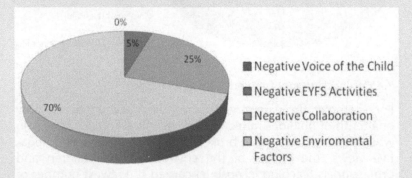

Figure 7.6 Negative comments by coding category

A five year old child asked her teacher during her maths lesson why the girl next to her was crying. Her teacher told her it was because she was having a procedure performed. The girl then asked if she was going to have a procedure, her teacher reassured her that she did not need one at that time. However, it was apparent that she was then pre-occupied with the thought of a procedure and the maths lesson was stopped in favour of a colouring activity.

One teacher suggested in her questionnaire response that moving children out of their bed-space and into the classroom provided an environment more conducive to learning. Having observed the spaces available for learning there was a significant discrepancy between the quality of spaces for teenagers and young people and areas for children in the early or primary years. For example, the teenage rooms in both hospitals were no more than four years old, with colourful and contemporary furniture, modern conveniences such as drinks machines, entertainment systems and large amounts of natural light. By comparison, the facilities for younger children were much smaller, darker and out-dated. Neither room for the younger children contained any convenience facilities or areas for relaxation. This suggests that learning spaces for children in their early years are not given the same level of consideration or funding as young adults.

Another factor to consider was the Ofsted report from the hospital school. This was completed in 2008 and rated the school as Outstanding. However, when the inspector visited the hospital school there were no children in early years on the register, therefore the provisions for early years were not rated and have not been checked since. This raises concerns about how staff view early years teaching and whether the same high standard of teaching is provided …

Analysis

This chapter will aim to answer the original research question posed by drawing upon the large body of evidence gained from literature, practical experience and research results. As stated in the methodology the ethical values of this research are deontological, and suggestions for additional research will be mentioned to further improve services for children who are in hospital.

The original areas for investigation were the latent conflict between the child's autonomy as an active participant in their care versus the medical law, and the challenge of meeting the early years' assessments targets. Initial interpretation of the literature and documentation did not fully take into consideration how multi-faceted this conflict is. For example, in relation to the child's medical needs, the law (Fraser/Gillick competency) is implicit that children under the age of 13 are not competent enough to make decisions that affect their care (Perera, 2007: 13). This contradicts the ethos of the hospital school who afford the children a great deal of choice and freedom of speech. However, evidence from findings shows that EYFS was valued 5% higher than the voice of the child, showing that the priority is still the curriculum. This highlights a further area of conflict, which is to what extent do the children feel confident to act as individuals in a hospital setting, and does this change according to the member of staff present?

One study researching the best practices for providing inclusive early childhood environments found that 'an image of early childhood programs in which most respondents viewed children as active participants working toward independence with individualized adaptations and with related services provided as a part of children's daily activities within a general education curriculum' (Hurley and Horn, 2010: 344) produced the most successful outcomes. On a basic level this was provided by the

Continues

Continued

hospital school. The school provided daily activities such as cooking, literacy and numeracy 'within a general education curriculum'. The school also provided 'individualized adaptations' through the hospital profile form. Evidence from observations and interviews with staff proved the use of hospital forms individual target setting helped to meet the needs of each child and areas of the curriculum.

Indeed, the expertise of the teaching staff in responding to the individual needs of the children were noted. One teacher stated that she 'adapts the lessons as [she] goes along to meet the child's needs'. This shows a high level of intuition and confidence. It also brings into question the barriers of working to a fixed curriculum. Teachers from the child's mainstream school are asked to send over their teaching plans to provide continuity of care, however, these plans are designed to be used in a classroom and therefore might not be suitable for use in hospital. It is to the credit of the teaching staff that these plans can be adapted to meet the needs of the child. Although this is responding to individual needs it is not necessarily encouraging children to 'work towards independence' (Hurley and Horn, 2010: 344) …

Commentary

Although Catherine says that she will first consider the results of the questionnaires, she does not only do this, but triangulates these results with the findings from her observations and interviews. Catherine's analysis effectively reaches positive conclusions about what she has observed, although areas for improvement are noted. This embodies the spirit of appreciative inquiry which is central to practitioner research. Catherine clearly brings her own perspective and her own judgements to her analysis. Here we return to Barab and Squire's (2004: 10) 'challenge' of making 'credible and trustworthy assertions' when the researcher is emotionally involved with the topic. We would expect all student practitioners to feel a passion for the topic that they have chosen to investigate; therefore all will hold a 'vested interest' in the outcome. Virtually all research which involves individuals and behaviours will be interpretive. Ultimately, Catherine has presented her own interpretation of the data that she has collected in order to improve her own understanding of the subject, and we can expect no more of a piece of practitioner research.

Consider this citation:

Qualitative writers are off the hook, so to speak. They don't have to try to play God, writing as disembodied omniscient narrators claiming universal, atemporal general knowledge; they can eschew the questionable metanarrative of scientific objectivity and still have plenty to say as situated speakers, sub-jectivities engaged in knowing/telling about the world as they perceive it. (Richardson, 1998: 348)

What are your thoughts?

 Key points from the chapter

- Always start by submerging yourself in the data that you have collected and give consideration to all key points that emerge – not just those that you were hoping to see.
- Code and sort your data under those key headings.
- Compare and contrast your different sources of data, do not be afraid to explore contradictions.
- Use strong examples from your data that support the point that you are making. Give data the chance to 'speak for itself'.

Further reading

Anderson, T. and Shattuck, J. (2012) Design-based research: a decade of progress in education research? *Educational Researcher,* 41(1): 16–25.
 This provides an interesting discussion in researcher bias.
Bell, J. (2010) *Doing Your Research Project: A Guide for First Time Researchers in Education, Health and Social Science.* 5th edn. Buckingham: Open University Press.
 This book offers clear practical support in analysing quantitative data.
Radnor, H. (2002) *Researching Your Professional Practice.* Buckingham: Open University Press.
 Radnor discusses the analysis of your data and how to seek out relationships and patterns.

8 Reaching conclusions and reflecting

In this chapter we will consider:

- The importance of considering your key findings and reaching conclusions;
- How you should reflect on the process of your research and what you have learned through carrying it out;
- The necessity of making clear the ways in which the research will impact upon your professional practice and, potentially, the practices of the setting;
- How you should identify areas for future research.

It is quite disconcerting how many textbooks overlook this step in the process of developing a research project, when we consider that it is this section which demonstrates just what you are able to take away from the whole research experience. In general, guidance tends to jump straight from analysing your data, to 'writing up your research project'. There seems an implication that once you have analysed your data you are done. This is characteristic of the 'research for research's sake' approach, as opposed to research that is directly focused upon bringing about change. As reflective practitioners we realise that the discoveries that emerge from your data are not an end point, instead this new knowledge is the starting point for future development. Considering 'where am I now and where will I go next?' is the crux of your research project.

It is no surprise that McNiff (2010), on the other hand, dedicates almost a third of her textbook, *Action Research for Professional Development*, to considering the significance of your findings and what you do with that information. McNiff (2010: 111) views it as vital to be able to clearly state what conclusions reflecting on your research has led you to if you are to create 'new discourses and debates about how your profession may move forward, and what pathways it might take'. But McNiff also adds a warning, not to take these conclusions as final and set in stone, but to remember that our knowledge is always in a state of flux. Knowledge is temporary; it will be modified by your next discovery. McNiff (2010: 106) reminds us of the humility with which we should approach our research, saying: 'You should always hold onto your knowledge lightly, and be aware that what you know today may change tomorrow. Always remember that you may, after all, be mistaken'. Research is an ongoing process of investigation and challenge to existing thinking.

Harriet gives an effective example of how she considered the key findings from her research in her study of role play and the home corner. She says:

> According to a detailed analysis of the data, it appeared that the 'meaningful' play experience of a domestic nature supported children's social capacity in a role-play situation. For instance, the re-enactment of familiar adult roles and situations from the immediate cultures of children were implemented and familiar and flexible play props were used. These gave children access to social and communication opportunities as is clear from the data. Additionally, the way in which children could use their home language with other children of the same linguistic background appeared to give them the confidence to develop their social play.
>
> This 'meaningful' notion supported my preconceived idea about role-play in a multicultural context having worked with children from varying cultures in Asia prior to this study where the importance of 'family' is a significant part of many eastern heritages. Children's clear interest in domestic 'family' play themes which potentially embrace familiarity for children is therefore relevant given that a large population of children in this study originate from Asian backgrounds. However, it was apparent that only specific children play in the home corner and thereby not all children benefit socially from the experience. As can be seen in the data, this issue concerns mainly male children. Consequently, it is possible to suggest that a new role-play area could be designed to be consistent with the interests of boys within the setting. Owing to the success of 'meaningful contexts' for children in this study, male children could be consulted with regards to the sort of role-play area that they would like to occupy as an additional space to the 'home corner.' This is then more likely to ensure that male children can access the same benefits from pretence play that many females currently achieve via the 'home corner' including the prospect of sharing, negotiation and co-operation.

In this excerpt Harriet clearly sets out what impact her study has had upon her understanding of this topic. One aspect of this it that the ideas she brought to this study (presented within her theoretical framework, see Chapter 2) were affirmed through the data that she collected. In acknowledging this she brings her research around full circle, 'At the beginning I had a hunch that this was the case and my data corroborated with this'. But she also demonstrates where she has developed new understandings through carrying out the research and how these might impact upon her future practice. She already felt that role play could have a positive influence upon the social development of children from culturally diverse backgrounds, but what she had not considered was the fact that this was predominantly accessed by girls. If it could be so beneficial then how could practitioners enable boys to access it more? It is at this point that Harriet begins to synthesise her learning from this experience (consulting with children to develop meaningful contexts) with her ideas for future research. She has developed a new question to tackle: 'If we consult boys as to what they would like developed as a role play opportunity, will they access it more frequently?'.

Consider your research more like a spiral than a cycle. You started at one point and then came back to reflect upon your original thoughts, but from a slightly different (and enlightened) angle. On comparing your new knowledge to your previous thoughts you then continue on a slightly different path.

How would you label the diagram in Figure 8.1?

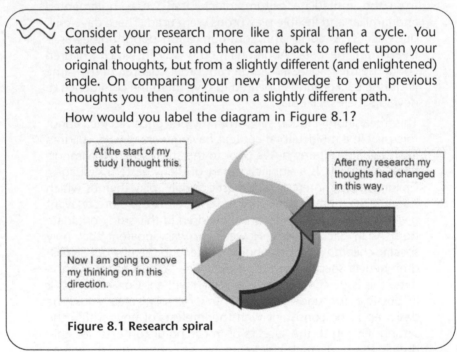

Figure 8.1 Research spiral

In her conclusions Harriet reflects not only upon her learning about the topic, but also upon how her understanding of research processes has developed. This is vital if you are to consider yourself (as you should) as a practitioner researcher in your future career. As we have already discussed in the Introduction, we are already researchers; we look for evidence all the time to clarify our understanding. But if we are able to collect and present that research in a structured and valid way, then we are in a stronger position to pass that information on. If some new knowledge has helped you, then it is likely to help others, so it should be shared.

Harriet says:

> In critique of this study, a reliance on qualitative methods and data collection exposed a difficulty in presenting results that were reliable and valid as the information could not be easily generalised or applied to alternative settings or research projects (Burton and Bartlett, 2009). However, the use of theory to support research findings (Yin, 1994, cited in Bassey, 1999) and the authenticity of the data supported the production of valid and reliable research claims (Bell, 2010). Also, the use of triangulation in this research; the application of a variety of research methods to confirm and support each other has enhanced reliability and validity (Cohen et al., 2007 and Yin, 2011). In order to overcome this issue in future research, I intend to adopt a more varied approach by making use of both qualitative and quantitative methods so that statistics can support narrative and descriptive data and consequently, avoid problems originally presented in 'generalising' to create conclusive claims (O'Leary, 2004). On reflection, questionnaires for a variety of practitioners may have supported this study where greater statistical analysis could have surfaced. Furthermore, striving to seek a greater sample of children for child conferencing interviews would have supported more reliable and valid results (Roberts-Holmes, 2005). However, this was reliant upon children's agreement to participate as a feature of informed consent, thus, could also present a barrier in the future where children may decide to not be a part of a research sample.

In the above paragraph Harriet acknowledges the weaknesses and strengths of her chosen research methods. My own research supervisor described this as 'limitations and delimitations', and this is a phrase that has stuck and that I now use with my own students. Within this section Harriet also discusses the concept of generalisability, something that is often raised as problematic within context-bound research. Previously I would have tried to justify the uniqueness of case studies by saying that you could use your results to come to the type of 'fuzzy generalisations' that Bassey first discussed in 1998. Bassey suggested that although it was impossible to surmise that the results that you have collected would apply to all similar settings, it is *possible* that they would apply to at least some. Therefore you were able to formulate a 'fuzzy generalisation'. I would not be so inclined to use this phraseology now, because I think that we are again trying to fit a square peg into a round hole in order to comply with positivist research convention. Practitioner research is specific to individuals and situations, so it cannot be generalised, but that does not stop the potential for others to learn from it and apply it to their own contexts. An example of this is that I found Bloor's (2010) brief discussion about the need to do 'good' in social research inspiring, even though it focused on research in a hospital, something that I have never experienced. I still found the concepts raised by Bloor fascinating, and those concepts were universally applicable. More credit needs to be given for the capacity of individuals to learn from the research experiences of others, even though that research experience may be based within an entirely different social context. No two settings are the same, no two research projects are the same, but that does not stop the potential for a positive impact to come about from it. We cannot generalise with results from our individual research but we can inspire others to contemplate and to question. If a piece of research motivates the researcher to take further action then it has been worthwhile; if it encourages just one other person to modify practice, then it has been successful. The worth of research should not be judged by its generalisability; that would be akin to judging the quality of food in a restaurant by its number of customers, and if we consider the popularity of mass produced fast food chains, then we know that is not the case.

 Consider some key messages that your study conveys that anyone within the field of early years childcare might learn from. For example, Harriet discovered how important it was to consult with children in order to provide 'meaningful contexts'. What concepts have come to light through your study which might be useful for fellow practitioners to consider?

Harriet comments that this research may have been improved by taking an approach that combined both quantitative and qualitative data, but it would have been useful for her to explore exactly the format that this data collection might have taken in a little more depth. She mentions using questionnaires, but what sort of questions could she have asked that resulted in quantitative data? Would quantitative data tracking the children's actual use of the home corner have helped, especially considering the comments made referring to the predominance of girls using the resource? Try to consider the detail of improvements that might have been made to your study.

At the end of your study careful thought needs to be given to exactly how the research could have been improved and sweeping statements about methods or sample size avoided. It is almost guaranteed that a number of studies finish with: 'In order to improve the study next time I would use a larger sample'. Please reflect more deeply than this; thoroughly explore the type of data that you collected and whether it provided sufficient information. Did you ask the right questions and in the right way? Did you record the right data during your observations? If response to your request for data was poor, do you think that you approached your research partners for the data collection in the right way? How could research relationships be improved next time? These are the types of ruminations that show that you have truly reflected upon the effectiveness of your research approaches. Unfortunately, some students believe that it will be a sign of failure to point out where they could have improved things (Mukherji and Albon, 2010) but this could not be further from the truth. McNiff (2010: 151) advises that you should 'write in a thoughtful way that shows your capacity for self-critique and your openness to the critique of others'. Recognising flaws in your research approaches proves that you have genuinely taken time to critically reflecting upon the whole experience, (just as you are continually expected to do as an early years practitioner), and that you have considered ways to make good practice even better in the future.

In the following excerpt from Harriet's conclusion, she discusses how the research has impacted upon her professionally. She says:

> As a developing practitioner of the early years, this research will be useful when supporting children from diversely cultural contexts which, as the introduction and rationale supports [sic], is expected to increase and so will be a prominent feature of early years and education practice of the future. This study has supported a personal understanding; that the creation of play spaces based on 'meaningful contexts' for children, including their unique cultures and interests, has the ability to enhance their play experience, development and, most prominently, their social development whilst learning English as an additional language.

This is a very effective example of making clear what you are able to take away from your study. I always tell students that conclusions are about reflecting on what has been achieved, but more importantly they are about what you will take forward: 'I have learned this and this is how it might affect my future practice'. As practitioners, the impact upon practice, and ultimately the impact upon the quality of the experience for the child, should always be at the forefront. This should be demonstrated in the conclusions that you reach.

Leanne (below) gives a strong example of how, in developing your own understanding through your research you can also impact upon practice within your setting. Sometimes students find it confusing that we stress that the focus of their research should be self-improvement, and then ask students to explain what impact this might have upon the setting. Sometimes struggle to see how these two things are interconnected. I do not explain this point nearly as well as McNiff (2010), who uses the analogy of a garden. She says that if we plant even one new flower in our garden it will alter the biosphere in some (albeit small) way. This garden is like the public spheres in which we live and work. Although we may feel powerless at times, we all have an influence upon those spheres, if only in a minimal way. The way that we act, the questions that we ask, will all impact upon that public space. By aiming to improve our own practice we can, potentially, have a positive impact upon those around us. McNiff (2010: 132) says, 'If you can make your action enquiry public, and produce an account to show how you tried to improve one small aspect of your work, you stand some hope of influencing the thinking of someone somewhere'. If you disseminate your findings to your colleagues, or others with whom you share your working sphere (as is discussed further in Chapter 9), then there is the possibility that your own discoveries could bring about change for the better. Below Leanne demonstrates how her study not only impacted upon her own understanding, but also gave a focus of development for herself and her colleagues.

Space and time for interesting and fun activities should be provided in order to facilitate self-directed learning. Carrying out regular observations provides vital opportunities to observe children's interests and cater for their individual needs. Appleby and Andrews (2012) say that reflective thinking leads to reflective learning. By reflecting on this issue, reading the literature and looking at it from my colleagues' lens, I have discovered that we do not observe enough. Other practitioners share the same view. As a team we need to decide what reflective action needs to take place in order to make improvements.

I have learnt that the balance of child initiated activities depends on the practitioners' pedagogical approach which changes depending on the context, child and staff. Therefore when I am in my role as a teacher I will need to use my own judgement and knowledge of each child to assess the children's individual needs from observations. This will give me more confidence in deciding what the appropriate balance should be. Discussions with colleagues enabled me to learn from their advice and experience. My study kept evolving. McNiff and Whitehead (2009) point out that your research question and thinking will be refined as your analysis deepens due to reading, reflection and discussion. After evaluating my issue from different lenses the focus has changed to:

How can staff ensure that they provide time for observations to be carried out on a regular basis?

This demonstrates that my story is on-going. This research inquiry has generated more questions that can lead to more investigations being carried out to further improve aspects of practice.

As we discussed earlier (Chapter 1), and as McNiff (2010: 136) stresses, 'any answers immediately transform into new questions'. A sometimes frustrating by-product of academic study is that the more we find out, the more we realise that we do not know. Because of this any study should conclude by recognising potential areas for future research. It is not uncommon for studies to recognise the need for future research in general, but not to specify exactly what form this research should take. This suggests a limited understanding of the function and possibilities of research. It is a little like saying 'I recognise that I need further training' without specifying exactly what type of training would be most beneficial to you. It is commendable that Harriet is very specific about the direction that she would like her further research to take in the excerpt below:

> This project has stimulated my interest in a potential future research initiative; particularly based on the impact of 'meaningful contexts' for children. As well as in a role-play environment, it would be significant to discover information about this concept on a wider scale throughout a variety of learning opportunities within the early years setting to find out if it holds the same relevance in other school-based activities for young children. Subsequently, the aim of this research would be to strengthen my practice as a whole and to seek greater knowledge concerning 'meaningful contexts' in the early childhood sector which has proved effective in this project.

Catherine, who explored the quality of the educational provision for young children in hospital, also pinpointed a specific area for future investigation:

> The transition from hospital school back to mainstream school or home tutoring would be another area of interest. As many children with chronic illness spend time in and out of hospital providing continuity of care would be key to them passing assessments and retaining a high level of education. This would require further ethical consideration as it would mean the researcher entering the child's home and/or mainstream school.

In doing so, Catherine recognises the further ethical issues that this area would bring with it, in juggling multiple contexts of research.

What questions has your study raised that would be interesting foci for future research? Do you wish to delve more deeply into your original area of research, do you wish to take it off on a tangent or has your research raised an entirely new area of interest?

Finally, we will spend some time looking at Nikki's concluding section to her study which looked at how a children's centre worked with parents. This example draws all of the elements that we have so far explored together, and so is included almost in full, with some very minor omissions:

The first and most significant finding regarding the investigation was the differing perceptions regarding the 'Time to Talk' (TTT) questionnaires. The differing opinions of the Children's Centre (CC) interviewees and parents illustrated confusion. For the CC practitioners the questionnaires are a very important and valuable tool to working in partnership with parents. Yet parents did not associate them as an approach to working in partnership, nor comprehend the value of the questionnaires. On discovering the parents' views after the focus group I reflected upon their opinions and could understand why they held them. The CC had the TTT questionnaires on the reception desk and also placed amongst other leaflets around the CC. Yet they did not promote them and there were no explanations as to why they are so valuable. **Therefore my first recommendation is to address this. The CC needs to advertise the questionnaires and not just display findings when they have been analysed. The questionnaires should be prominently displayed and promoted and used as part of the working in partnership display approach, which I shall discuss further in the next recommendation.**

Discovering that CC practitioners and parents using the CC were all in favour of developing working in partnership was promising. This conclusion was reached by the parents' comment that initiated the directional change of the research; by parents expressing shared opinions during the focus group of how they would like to engage more with the CC and by practitioners recognising that in order to provide parents with services that are needed and wanted they must facilitate ways that parents can voice their needs and wants. This was exceedingly positive and illustrated that when practitioners and parents engage in a mutually respectful relationship then working in partnership is possible (Ward, 2009, Rodd, 2009). With this united feeling towards working in partnership in mind **the second recommendation would be developing displays within the CC that demonstrate a 'Working in Partnership with Parents' approach. Such displays may include: a parent's policy or charter; how the CC aims to engage parents; how parents are valued: why the CC wants to work in partnership with parents. For the parents to feel they have a voice within the CC I would suggest the CC implements a parent notice board and parents' suggestion box.** These would demonstrate how the CC respects parents, their ideas and values their contributions (Knopf and Swick, 2007). In turn this would contribute to empowering parents (Williams, 2008). These ideas were raised with the CC manager and colleagues after the interviews and were welcomed positively.

The Parents' Notice Board and suggestion box have since been implemented and are proving to be very successful. Parents have been putting ideas up for local events and offering tips for toys that are currently popular and the suggestion box has had ideas for activities put into it and suggestions for possible toys that the CC might consider buying. Whilst both offer anonymity to parents (since they are not required to put their names on items), the suggestion box also provides parents who are less confident with writing ideas down, more privacy, as these suggestions are only viewed by the CC practitioners (if the parent has worries regarding their spelling or handwriting they are happy to put ideas in the box as it will not be viewed publicly).

The third recommendation would be the CC establishes a crèche. Both the CC interviewees and parents during the interviews recognised that having a crèche would certainly facilitate opportunities for working in partnership. Regardless of whether parents wanted to become more involved with the CC, many were unable to because they had no childcare. Therefore the only solution to allow for parents to engage in parent forums, or participate in interviewing or consultations would be daytime meetings offering crèche facilities.

Since carrying out the interviews and the focus group a crèche has been introduced as a permanent weekly service. The crèche was a crucial element identified by all potential partners in the partnership and has certainly impacted upon facilitating

Continues

Continued

parental involvement. Furthermore it has demonstrated to parents that the CC is listening to them.

The fourth recommendation having considered some of the parents' comments during the focus group would be that the CC allows parents to actively participate during sessions if they wish to. Two parents in particular wanted to be able to help the practitioner by carrying out activities and generally supporting the children's learning during sessions (Pugh and De'Ath, 1989). Conversely, other parents, although liking the principle of the idea, felt their confidence might hinder participation of this nature. This illustrated that every parent will have their own idea of the degree they would like to become engaged with the partnership. Therefore the CC must respect the parent's choice regarding their level of engagement, yet also implement strategies for those wishing to participate at such a supportive level ... if the CC promotes partnership and encourages parental involvement it may well encourage more parents to have confidence to engage in some participation. Consequently this could encourage parents to have a sense of being an effective member of the CC and one who engages in helping create the environment (Knopf and Swick, 2007).

The fifth recommendation relates to parents providing feedback for the individual sessions. Despite verbal feedback being a popular choice for parents and CC practitioners this cannot realistically be the only option, since the CC is accountable to Ofsted. Therefore the CC needs to consider having activity feedback sheets in the playroom next to the various activities and toys which are in a tick style format as these are less time consuming for parents and they would be anonymous, unless the parent wrote things down too.

... Undertaking this study has impacted on me both personally and professionally. Personally my knowledge regarding working in partnership with parents and engaging them in shaping services has been considerably developed, and I have enjoyed reading the literature surrounding the subject. Professionally, I feel privileged to have been given the opportunity to carry out the research, and also that everyone who contributed to the research did so willingly and honestly. The transparency of the

CC meant I was able to look closely at the current practices regarding this concept and consider how it may be developed. Carrying out the interviews meant I was able to compare opinions, seek similarities and consequently propose realistic recommendations that would enhance current practice. I believe that practitioners working at the CC and parents attending will see the benefits that the research has brought.

If I were to carry out this study again I would seek to gain more experience regarding interviews. Despite using structured questions which are ideal for novice researchers (Bell, 1999), I felt my inexperience with interviewing was a disadvantage. This was particularly evident during the focus group, which at times lost direction. Whilst information provided was useful, at times returning to the issue with the parents was difficult; a more experienced interviewer would probably have managed this better. Having more participation with the questionnaires would be the next improvement I would strive for. Although the data gathered was insightful regarding the initial focus, once the investigation evolved, it would have been useful to seek parents' individual perceptions regarding working in partnership. This could then have been followed up within the focus group but time restraints would not have allowed this to happen. Also parents may not have wanted to complete another questionnaire, and then engage in a focus group, especially as there was no permanent crèche at this point. Hence childcare would have been an issue.

However Koshy (2005: 122) offers an assurance regarding these niggles as he makes the point:

'Remind yourself that the mode of study that you have selected is action research and the purpose is ... to improve practice or implement change for the purpose of professional development. The intention of the action research is not to make generalisable claims, but to tell a story which is of interest to other practitioners who may want to learn from it'.

I believe the investigation has changed and developed existing practices in my workplace. Furthermore I have developed personally and professionally as a consequence of carrying it out. I believe in future as a professional I will never take lightly the concept of working in partnership with parents and recognise that establishing respectful relationships is a crucial element to engaging parents in shaping services.

You will notice that Nikki's conclusions take a different approach to Harriet's reflections. She does not discuss her key findings as such, but presents recommendations. Nikki suggests very concrete and useful 'solutions' to the problems highlighted, which, I must stress, is not always necessary. As practitioner research is predominantly about your personal development, making recommendations may not always be appropriate. More often consideration of how you might modify your own future practice is far more relevant than suggesting that others modify theirs. But it would seem, from Nikki's study, that the children's centre was very open to ideas and that the advice given was received warmly. You will know best what is most suitable within your own research context. In the next chapter we look in more detail at how results should be fed back to research participants and to settings.

In conclusion, it is important not to 'skip over' this aspect of a study as it contains valuable information and reflections upon your research project as a whole. Here you summarise your findings and what you can take away from the project. You also consider, as Nikki did so disarmingly when she reflected on her interviews, what did not go as you would have liked and how it might be improved next time. Consider what needs to be included in the conclusion to your study by answering the following questions:

 Key points from the chapter

- What key themes or ideas emerged from your data analysis?
- How did these relate back to your original thoughts (found in your theoretical framework) and to the theories of others that you explored in your literature review?
- How was the data that you collected limited? What valuable insights can you still take away from it?
- Reflecting on the research process, what went well, what did not and what would you change next time?
- How will the knowledge that you have gained through carrying out this research impact upon your future practice?
- Has this research impacted in any way upon the setting?
- What new questions has this research raised that you might like to explore in the future?

Further reading 📖

Bloor, M. (2010) The researcher's obligation to bring about good, *Qualitative Social Work*, 9(11): 17–20. Available at: www. sagepublications.com; DOI: 10.1177/1473325009355616 (accessed 14 December 2012).
This gives an example of the multidisciplinary nature of research and how we can learn from studies conducted in very different contexts.
McNiff, J. (2010) *Action Research for Professional Development*. Poole: September Books.
Discusses the importance of reflecting upon the new knowledge that your research has generated for you and how you will move forward using this in the future.
Mukherji, P. and Albon, D. (2010) *Research Methods in Early Education. An Introductory Guide*. London: Sage.
This text encourages you to reflect critically upon the research process and to consider improvements you might make to it.

9 Disseminating findings

This chapter:

- Uses the reflections from the students on what doing the research meant for them personally, its impact on practice and their wider learning;
- Draws together the themes of the other chapters;
- Highlights key messages arising from the studies;
- Looks at how research findings are used to inform practice or circulated to a wider audience;
- Asks students to consider various ways in which they can share their findings with their colleagues so that the research takes on a meaning beyond the independent study.

Introduction

As your research project draws to a close and you reflect back on the journey you have taken, hopefully you will realise that your piece of work makes a unique contribution to the body of knowledge within early years practice. You have, as McNiff (2011) tells us, ventured into the unknown and developed new insights which will not have a finite ending as you hand in your study. The journey that you have taken is likely to continue beyond your university course into your future practice and, in order to follow through this process, the results of your study should be fed back and discussed with settings and if possible with the wider community of practice, for example your local authority and colleagues. Throughout this book, we have stressed the importance of purpose within your project and adopted a praxeological approach to research as being immediately available for settings to use (Pascal and

Bertram, 2012c). It is from the existing body of knowledge within the setting that new insights into practice can be constantly developing. Just as we make discoveries about children's learning through our observations and following the child's interests closely, and develop new ways of being and learning with children to maximise their potential, we can do the same with our research and use it with others to make a difference.

However, if we are to give full attention to the importance of disseminating results, this process needs to start right at the beginning of the study, with your design. In order to ensure ethical practice, you will need to tell your participants at the outset how you will feed back your findings to them and decide who you will involve and how you will communicate with them. In other words, the actions from your research may occur at the end but the process of dissemination starts at the beginning. This consideration will help to authenticate your research by giving credence to your motivation in carrying out the research and establishing your values to the reader and the participants. At each stage of the project, you will need to consider this aspect of your work as you develop, design and carry out your research and, as such, dissemination is an incremental process leading to a final product. As Nolan et al. (2013) suggest, it is a good idea to begin writing for dissemination during the early stages of the research following the logical order of the study.

It may well be that sometimes the dissemination of the findings becomes part of your research. For example, if you are observing a child as part of your study on risky play and that child falls off the slide, it would be unethical to just stand by and watch, as Bloor (2010) discusses in his work. You will act to help the child and inform staff, and this then may become part of your research findings. In this way, sometimes dissemination can become blurred by ethical responsibility.

Figure 9.1 shows the stages of consideration of dissemination and is represented as a circular process reflecting the ongoing nature of research within constantly developing practice.

In the previous chapter we looked at how Harriet draws our attention to the potential of her research to support children from diverse cultures and to lead on to further research. She reflected upon her work into how the 'home corner' of a multicultural early childhood setting used for the purposes of role play impacts on the social development of young children. Harriet identifies how she would like her research to continue in order to develop her knowledge and practice in this area and through this promote understanding of this important aspect of practice. The very wealth of information and understandings that you uncover are worth celebrating not only at the end of the process but also at various stages throughout. For example, as Figure 9.1 indicates, the literature reviewed is useful to discuss with colleagues, participants and others as it broadens knowledge and informs practice as well as updating potentially busy professionals who do not always have time to read and research in the same way. This can take place during the process or after and can be done in a variety of ways.

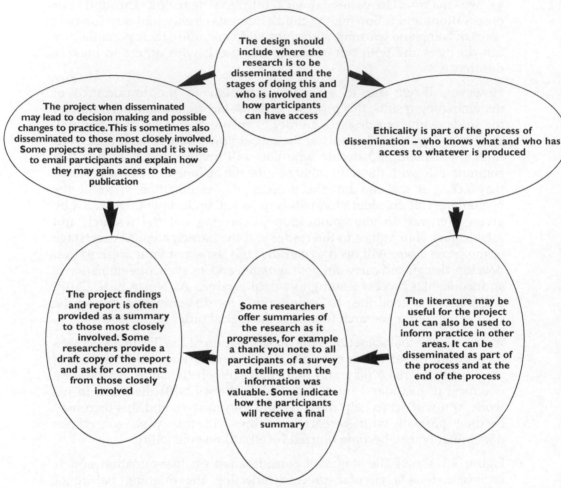

The design should include where the research is to be disseminated and the stages of doing this and who is involved and how participants can have access

The project when disseminated may lead to decision making and possible changes to practice. This is sometimes also disseminated to those most closely involved. Some projects are published and it is wise to email participants and explain how they may gain access to the publication

Ethicality is part of the process of dissemination – who knows what and who has access to whatever is produced

The project findings and report is often provided as a summary to those most closely involved. Some researchers provide a draft copy of the report and ask for comments from those closely involved

Some researchers offer summaries of the research as it progresses, for example a thank you note to all participants of a survey and telling them the information was valuable. Some indicate how the participants will receive a final summary

The literature may be useful for the project but can also be used to inform practice in other areas. It can be disseminated as part of the process and at the end of the process

Figure 9.1 Stages of dissemination of research

Harriet, in researching with children, could have considered feeding back to the children involved in her research. Mukherji and Albon (2010: 246) point out that as we become accustomed to working with the children we can sometimes forget the importance of sharing our findings with them. They suggest that one method may be to compile a book of photographs during the research to be used '*with*' and '*for*' the children.

Emily chose to disseminate her findings on a number of levels. She, along with other students from her cohort, was concerned that her independent study should not merely be put away to gather dust. She hoped that other settings besides her own could benefit not only from the findings but also from the research design, knowledge from the literature reviews and the approach taken to ethicality. She reflects back on her study and learning:

It was important for me to identify if changes and policy development may have had any effect upon the staff working at the centre and if there has been any impact upon the children and families in the community which it serves. The data presented within the results are not intended to provide sweeping generalizations about how all staff at the centre feel, or indeed how all children's centres across the country may be affected at this time of national change. Rather I have hopefully been able to provide a subjective account, which has possibly provoked thought and discussion between colleagues at the centre.

The current political issues surrounding Sure Start Children's Centres is cause for huge debate. Therefore, the subject choice for my study was perhaps not the easiest to undertake for my first small scale research project. The size and scope of issues which have been uncovered has meant that it has been a challenge to maintain focus. My qualitative study using a variety of approaches has collected a wide amount of data, only a sample of which I have been able to include in this study. During my research I have learnt a lot about leadership and management which was perhaps not completely expected. I have been able to identify the effects of inspirational leadership which has motivated staff and brought cohesiveness to the team despite uncertain times. I feel that I have been able to meet my aims and also perhaps identified issues for future research and consideration.

Commentary

Emily became part of a group of students who came together as a writing group to edit, publish and share the results of their investigations for an audience within their own local authority. Influenced by the work of Wenger (1998; Wenger et al., 2002) they formed a community of practice with a remit of mutual engagement, joint enterprise and shared repertoires. They effectively carried out this work together with an agreed purpose, shared expectations and shared experience as well as finding strategies to solve problems. Wenger (1998: 58) saw this as a way of 'giving form to our experience – producing objects that congeal this experience into thingness'. Thus, Emily's work was recognised as a solid foundation for understanding the current situation for staff within children's centres and beyond this to the wider local area.

The students, including Emily, produced a booklet which was funded by the local authority for dissemination to all the settings in the area and for use with future students undertaking their work-based inquiry. It contained a collection of research summaries, including literature reviews and photographs. Its writing style followed academic conventions and the layout used sub-headings and contained written extracts and sometimes diagrams taken from the original dissertations. It was well received and considered innovative by colleagues and the local authority. When Reed and Walker (2012) researched into this process they found that it was transformational for the participants. They took on roles of mentors and critical friends to others completing a degree and developed their skills as competent writers. As Le Gallais (2004) indicates, the students transformed what might seem like ordinary practice into something quite special.

As you can see, Emily's research was a subject for ongoing debate among professionals at the centre. Some researchers, as Figure 9.1 indicates, prefer to disseminate to participants throughout the research, perhaps with a positive acknowledgement of their participation. Others take the opportunity of a more formal feedback, as Leanne clearly demonstrates:

In this independent study I show how I developed my knowledge of child initiated learning. I tell the story of an action research investigation that was carried out in my setting. Bolton (2010) says that aspects of people's lives can be narrated as a story. The difference with my study is that there will be no definite end because it is a work based issue that is part of my life and is therefore ongoing.

As a result of my study I discovered new knowledge which I wanted to share with my colleagues. An early years meeting took place in my setting where I was able to feedback the findings of my investigation. Practitioners were able to comment on various aspects of the inquiry. McNiff (2002) refers to these as critical but creative conversations where everyone can learn from each other. In agreement with this is Bolton (2010) who believes that through this type of dialogue practitioners are able to share alternative perspectives and discuss potential amendments to future practice. The main area for discussion was that practitioners need to plan for more observations to take place on a regular basis.

When practitioners reflect critically Brookfield (1995) tells us that there can be disagreements. Some members of the early years team were able to see by the evidence from the observations and children's photographs and drawings how much I learnt about their individual interests. They were able to recognise the value and significance of these observations. We discussed how this could inform future planning. Other practitioners expressed their concerns that there is not always time to observe especially when targets have to be achieved. Appleby and Andrews (2012) point out that this is because staff have diverse principles and beliefs. Some practitioners have different priorities and this depends on their 'way of being' in practice. The Foundation Stage leader advised staff that in September when the new intake start more time should be allocated for them to make regular observations in order to become familiar with new children and identify their interests. A new observation recording sheet is also being devised.

Commentary

Leanne shows us here how she discussed her work with her colleagues and acknowledges the continuing journey of her research as a part of her professional life. As an ethically sensitive early years practitioner, Leanne has made a commitment to form authentic relationships with her participants and to engage in critically reflective dialogue with them in order that they became active participants in moving forward the issues raised by the research. She had to, however, come to an understanding of her values and her own learning first in order to share this with others. Her research was based on the development of a context which is respectful of her participants and understanding that as a result of her research, views will differ but that debate will be fostered and new practice will emerge.

MacNaughton (2004: 53) explains that research and the learning following on from this are never value free and involve ethics, values and politics within a 'dynamic of power'. In view of this the potential power imbalance between you as a researcher and your participants must be considered. Leanne has been sensitive to the nuances of power within the team both as a researcher and team member without authority to make changes.

Leanne considers the reactions of practitioners to her research and her position within the organisation. She identifies herself not as a manager or leader within the setting but she has been in a position to exert influence and show what McDowall Clark (2012: 399) terms as 'catalytic leadership.' She has made a commitment to professional development, taken small steps within her research to make incremental changes and supported others to discuss and to reflect on practice. She has therefore acted as a catalyst in 'bringing about quality improvement in early years settings through continual reflection and ongoing improvement'.

Walter et al. (2005) identify eight conditions favourable to the implementation of evidence-based practice. These include good translation of messages, ownership among users, enthusiastic facilitators, sensitivity to context, credibility, leadership, support and integration.

Can you see these conditions identified in the examples of the students' work?

As Figure 9.1 shows us, sometimes recommendations are made by projects which are taken up by the setting involved. This was the case in Nikki's research where she identified achievable changes to practice concerning partnership working with parents, which were put into place by the setting. These have been set out in full and the recommendations highlighted in bold in Chapter 8. In making recommendations and feeding these back it is important to bear in mind the appreciative stance of researching 'with' and not 'on' settings and to ensure that the positives as well as areas for improvements are highlighted. Catherine does this very effectively in her study:

The aim of this research thesis is to identify how the education, social and emotional needs of children in their early years are met whilst in hospital. The use of Government policies such as the Every Child Matters Agenda (ECM, England: DCSF, 2003) and the Early Years Foundation Stage (EYFS) (DfES, 2007) were tested alongside current literature and evidence from practice. A particular interest was taken in the collaborative practice of the play therapists and the teaching staff. The research was guided by a deontological approach and the best interests of the child were always considered and maintained. The results derived highlight best practice as well as areas that would increase autonomy and improve service provision for children who are in hospital. The most notable finding was the commitment of the staff to providing a caring and encouraging service. It was apparent that the teaching staff and the play therapists valued one another and recognised their joint contribution in caring for the child. Both recognised the strain and anxiety faced by children in hospital and responded to their needs in a holistic manner.

The analysis identified certain hospital school policies that worked well in the interests of the child, such as the Hospital Profile Form. The benefits of this procedure were that it recognised each child as an individual and established the initial collaboration with the child's mainstream school. The form also complies with the ECM Agenda and elements of the United Nations Convention on the Rights of the Child by using individual target setting and by being highly adaptable.

The versatility and creativity of both the teaching and play therapy professionals improved provision for the children and enabled a bespoke service to be provided for each child. It was clear from observations that the children enjoyed sessions with both professionals and viewed them as both a source of fun and comfort. A service which normalises and eases the stresses of a hospital stay cannot be overlooked.

The most significant findings were the need to provide play therapists with collaborative training from both the education and healthcare sectors; the need to improve play spaces in hospital for children in their early years and the need for multi-disciplinary working.

Similarly, Samantha wanted the opportunity to extend and develop a better community of practice by opening up the research process to a panel of participants that included all staff, representatives of parents, committee members and teachers. As she articulates, 'I am a true ambassador of community practice and believe "getting it right" isn't down to just one person or one body of professionals'. The staff, committee and parents formed the review panel where the results of the study were considered and the objective of producing documentation and training for parents detailing the children's learning journey for literacy within the setting. She writes:

Throughout the research process I did reflect on my ethicality as I was offering myself open as the manager for criticism. I was presented with data that conflicted with my understanding on how others have perceived the standards of education being developed within the setting. I prepared myself to be challenged by staff, parents, committee and other educating professionals. From researching ethics and experiencing an 'insider' position it can be a hard part of the project as your practice and management is open to criticism. It was important for me to take time to step back and analyse data, conversations as a whole and not individually. As mentioned earlier, I have always been an ambassador of building a community of practice and believe a collection of perspectives

Continues

Continued

provides a more effective process for continuing development. Sometimes it can provoke uncomfortable situations but through strong interpersonal skills this can be resolved. As an insider-researcher, I appreciated that I would go through a learning process that supported my reflective approach to the setting I manage and my learning with regards to work based projects.

Therefore, I was making an investment for quality improvement within the setting. Raelin (2008) recognised this growing body of evidence suggesting that work based projects may provide immensely beneficial to the long term success of companies.

This study departs from traditional evaluation practices where I the researcher evaluate the results singularly. I had the opportunity to observe a practical evaluation process through the review panel. Therefore in this section I will summarise the responses to the aims.

Within practice

Identify what techniques and strategies are used within the setting that encourages literacy skills.

• All participants agreed strongly that the variety of techniques and strategies do provide a good foundation for literacy development.

• It was agreed the visual display board that was used for the parents' information afternoon was to be adapted into a leaflet that would benefit being attached to the settings brochure pack.

How are the techniques and strategies managed and utilised within a flexible provision?

✗ Interestingly many parents found the systematic process of the circle time sessions confusing.

✗ The feedback from staff was that the six week/'half termly' time limit was not long enough especially when referring to the first half term of the year when settling is a priority.

√ It was agreed to extend these programmes for a whole term.

√ Parents added they would like more advertisement of these, so each term they could better select the sessions in response to the programme on offer.

Communication

Are parents aware of the techniques and strategies?

✗ The initial response from parents was no until the literacy afternoon.

√ All participants agreed that through the opportunity to have a literacy information afternoon was more effective and made the messages clearer instead of having to read letters or message boards.

√ It was agreed that this should be offered twice not once a year.

Is there enough evidence within children's learning journeys?

✗ It was agreed that the evidence within the learning journeys do not reflect the various opportunities that all children are experiencing.

✗ Staff agreed that it very time consuming constantly writing up everything and that the process needed to be reviewed.

√ Parents responded by articulating that with this additional support for literacy understanding it has re-set their understanding and that not everything can be documented which is not the important part, it was the fact that the children were experiencing these opportunities.

√ Staff responded by referring to the individual planning sheets that are on display in the classroom could document these experiences here. Using the learning journeys more specifically for observations and next steps of development instead of a diary.

Expectations

What are the expectations of parents regarding literacy skills?

√ All parents agreed from after the information afternoon they felt more relaxed and inspired with regard to literacy skills.

√ They appreciated the complexity of children's learning but felt that by doing what they referred to as the 'basics' of reading together, singing rhymes and just talking was so effective and fun!

√ They felt more informed and reassured on how it was well managed between the setting and the reception class within the whole EYFS journey.

In this project, we the community of participants held ourselves responsible for the success both of the project and its evaluation, therefore, the evaluation should not be seen as the evaluation of programmes so much as the evaluation of the people through whom programmes affect being directly the child, but just as importantly the parents; drawing on the work of Barry MacDonald (1985), where the evaluation 'should take the experience of program participants as the central focus of investigation'. Consequently we were investigating the experience of reflecting on our own work, which, as major contemporary theorists such as Bullough and Pinnegar (2001) say, is the main focus of an emergent tradition of self study.

Commentary

In this excerpt you can see not only that a series of recommendations were made but that the community of practice was involved in the dissemination of findings throughout the process. This enabled the objectives to be met and an evaluation of the way in which the community works together becomes an integral part of the process of research.

Other methods of dissemination of findings may include newsletters to staff or to parents, display boards within the setting, letters or cards. It is important to bear in mind your audience when considering these and to ensure that the language used is clear, straightforward and jargon free. Participants' needs are paramount here and a professional, sensitive approach bearing in mind any issues of ethicality, for example identification of participants in a small sample, should be borne in mind. Also, think through the length of your feedback and ask yourself what is likely to be of most interest to your participants and in what format would be best suited to their needs. Different content will be needed for different audiences who, as Fetterman (2010: 113) tells us, have different 'needs and concerns'. Your abstract for your study may be written as a form of giving feedback on the entirety of the project to participants but also to a wider audience, potentially even for publication or presentation at conferences.

 Key points from the chapter

In order to prompt you in considering this, Table 9.1 opposite, developed by Michael Reed (2013), highlights some ideas.

Further reading

Cullen, J., Hedges, H. and Bone, J. (2011) Planning, undertaking and disseminating research, in S. Callan and M. Reed (eds), *Work Based Research in the Early Years*. London: Sage.
    This chapter gives some pertinent questions to ask yourself when considering disseminating your research both to participants and other organisations.
Mukherji, P. and Albon, D. (2010) *Research Methods in Early Childhood*. London: Sage.
    This book gives advice on disseminating research findings with children, giving practical suggestions about how to do this stage appropriately.
Nolan, A., Macfarlane, K. and Cartmel, J. (2013) *Research in Early Childhood*. London: Sage.
    This book includes a chapter with guidance and questions to ask yourself when taking the journey through structuring feedback. It is particularly helpful in considering poster displays and oral feedback.

Table 9.1 Feedback summary

Nudge points to help you consider a summary of the inquiry for others to read or as a presentation	Nudge points to help you consider ways to show how the setting was involved. You may not use them all – they are there to nudge you towards a critical look back at what went on
General points	It is a summary of what went on, not the whole inquiry. Take care to be ethically correct and if you promised anonymity – keep to this. Write for your intended audience rather than reproduce an 'academic style' that may not be easily assimilated by those who read the summary. Include the date it was produced and indicate who it is intended for. You may care to reassure people that ethicality and care for children was a focus throughout. You may care to offer thanks to those involved for their cooperation.
The purpose, key themes and or questions that prompted you to start the inquiry	You may like to say how the focus was discussed with the setting, how the children and perhaps parents were involved/contributed.
What you did	Explain your approach: did this have an ethical base? Were you an active participant in the research process? Was it to do with why or how something works through gathering evidence and evaluating that evidence? Did it require critical self evaluation? It may be useful to say how you considered the views of published research and if this was valuable in helping you to understand the area you were investigating. Describe the process that you went through. This will help others to understand how you gathered evidence.
Sharing with others what you found	There may be areas of general applicability and interest. Rarely are there definite conclusions. It may be more like the inquiry (the evidence) allowed you to see things from a number of different viewpoints. Make clear what you found. Does it relate to a particular setting or context rather than attempting to make comparisons.
Professional and personal impact	It is valuable to say what you have learnt. For example, how the process helped your studies or had an influence on practice/your understanding/confidence as a researcher.

Final reflection on the qualities of a practitioner researcher

Our views within this book have been influenced by the work of Jacobson (1998), who discusses the open-ended nature of practitioner research, Reed (2013) in his encouragement of practitioner research, and McNiff (2011) who highlights the importance of the role of the researcher practitioner. Our own reflection on the content of this book allows us to argue that work-based learning should not be seen as detached from the rest of your learning as students as it is embedded in both your practice and studies throughout your early years experience. As we have sought to show throughout the book, research is an intrinsic part of daily practice through which practitioners are *constructing* knowledge within the learning and work environment. This process of research engages you in different phases of practice-based reflection: before an activity, when you do it and afterwards. It has the potential to allow you to explore and question practice and values within your environment with a view to enhancing and developing processes and procedures.

This book asks you as the researcher to consider not only what you are researching but the purpose and why this is important; to consider real-world 'collaborative inquiry' as a means to elicit views on what is happening and what works on the ground. In this way, your research will be of immediate value and use in the workplace and enrich understanding of practice to the ultimate benefit of children and families.

This form of practice-based inquiry inherently demonstrates personal and professional qualities which are increasingly known as professional dispositions; a term coined by Rike and Sharp (2008) when considering the qualities of young early years teachers. For a work-based researcher, Reed (2013) tells us they may be something like:

- the ability to provide a warm, caring and purposeful way of effectively researching with children, young people and families;

- being adept at sharing information, with other professionals;

- seeing the value of being part of multi-agency working;
- the ability to be curious about a child's development and wanting to improve practice from the ground up;
- see the research process as ethical – doing no harm to anyone involved and safeguarding the welfare of the child;
- see research as something which allows a reflection on practice and have a positive response to change;
- research with an open mindset that encourages a celebration of diversity and inclusion to promote the welfare of children;
- view continuing professional development as an important aspect of professional inquiry and practice.

Of course, it can be argued that such dispositions are no more than can be expected of any researcher in the field. However, it is our opinion that further considerations of the way practice-based research has to encompass a number of approaches should be taken into account. As a practice-based researcher you may be an insider within a setting and it will be important to make a significant and long-lasting contribution to improving practice. You (as an insider) are heavily accountable to others in the workplace and are motivated to engage ethically and rigorously in their investigations. You will be careful about accepting what you are told is good practice, and consequently compare and contrast the practice of others with what you see. You are concerned with inquiring into what works and why, asking what can be done to extend and improve practice. This book encourages you to see the process of research as just as valuable as the product and to underpin your research with your own personal and professional values and to have an ethical understanding of why and how your research may impact on children and families. It promotes understanding of the need for collected evidence to be clear, rounded and fit for purpose. It asks you to consider the audience and strive to share your findings with others honestly, including successes, failures, trials and tribulations, and to reflect and learn from the process. In doing so you are creating opportunities to form communities of practice (Wenger, 1998; Wenger et al., 2002) whereby you work with others on raising questions, finding solutions and developing quality experiences for young children.

Finally, in looking at the work of Jacobson (1998) and Reed (2013) we can conclude that:

- A practice-based researcher sees their role not as 'the' investigator but 'facilitating' an investigation (with others). They act with humility and care;
- A practice-based researcher sees their role as not only utilising methods to investigate practice but becoming integral to these;

- A practice-based researcher moves away from a theoretical inquiry into which meanings associated with educational experience and considers their own actions on, in and for practice;

- Practice-based researchers consider their position, the context, their actions, the research relevance, potential responses, consequences and ethicality as part of their research design. They consider the integrity of the data and their actions;

- A practice-based researcher can consider what is expected and what is happening 'on the ground'. Their actions are rooted in purpose, and they acknowledge constraints. They are able to 'test' theory in action. Process is as important as product, because the process of inquiring may lead to changes in practice.

References

Alderson, P. and Morrow, V. (2011) *The Ethics of Research with Children and Young People: A Practical Handbook*. London: Sage.

Anderson, T. and Shattuck, J. (2012) Design-based research: a decade of progress in education research? *Educational Researcher*, 41(1): 16–25.

Appleby, K. and Andrews, M. (2012) Reflective practice is the key to quality improvement, in Association of Colleges Annual Conference. Birmingham, England November 2012.

Astley, J. (2011) The vocation and virtues of research, paper presented at the Value and Virtue in Practice-Based Research Conference, York St John University, 1–2 June.

Aveyard, H. (2010) *Doing a Literature Review in Health and Social Care*. 2nd edn. Maidenhead: McGraw Hill.

Barab, S. and Squire, B. (2004) Design-based research: putting a stake in the ground, *Journal of the Living Sciences*, 13(1): 1–14.

Bassey, M. (1998) Fuzzy generalisation: an approach to building educational theory, paper presented at the BERA Annual Conference, The Queen's University of Belfast, 27–30 August.

Bell, J. (1993) *Doing Your Research Project: A Guide for First Time Researchers in Education and Social Science*. 2nd edn. Buckingham: Open University Press.

Bell, F. (1988) Reviewing the literature: a student's perspective, *Journal of Health Care*, 2: 122–7. Online at: http://chc.sagepub.com/content/2/3/122. (accessed 3 July 2012).

Bell, J. (2010) *Doing Your Research Project: A Guide for First Time Researchers in Education, Health and Social Science*. 5th edn. Buckingham: Open University Press.

Bloor, M. (2010) The researcher's obligation to bring about good. Vol. 9 (11): 17–20. Available from: sagepub.co.uk/journalsPermissions.nav, www.sagepublications.com DOI: 10.1177/1473325009355616.

British Association for Early Childhood (2011) *Code of Ethics*. Online at: http://www.early-education.org.uk/sites/default/files/Code%20of%20Ethics.pdf. (accessed 6 November 2012).

British Educational Inquiry Association (BERA) (2011) *Revised Ethical Guidelines for Educational Research*. Southwell: BERA. Online at: http://www.bera.ac.uk. (accessed 12 July 2013).

Bronfenbrenner, U. (1979) *The Ecology of Human Development: Experiments by Nature and Design*. Cambridge, MA: Harvard University Press.

Callan, S. and Reed, M. (eds) (2011) *Work-Based Research in the Early Years*. London: Sage.

Callan, S., Picken, L. and Foster, S. (2011) Ethical positioning in work-based investigations, in S. Callan and M. Reed (eds), *Work-Based Research in the Early Years*. London: Sage. pp. 17–31.

Carr, W. (2000) Partisanship in educational research, *Oxford Review of Education*, 26(3/4): 495–501.

Christensen, P. and Prout, A. (2002) Working with ethical symmetry in social research with children, *Childhood*, 9(4): 477–97.

Clark, A., Kjorholt, T. and Moss, P. (eds) (2005) *Beyond Listening: Children's Perspectives on Early Childhood Services*. Bristol: Policy Press.

Cohen, L., Manion, L. and Morrison, K. (1989) *Research Methods in Education*. London: RoutledgeFalmer.

Cohen, L., Manion, L. and Morrison, K. (2001) *Research Methods in Education*. 5th edn. London: RoutledgeFalmer.

Cohen, L., Manion, L. and Morrison, K. (2007) *Research Methods in Education*. 6th edn. London: RoutledgeFalmer.

Coolican, H. (1990) *Research Methods and Statistics in Psychology*. London: Hodder and Stoughton.

Cooperrider, D. (2005) *Appreciative Inquiry: A Positive Revolution in Change*. San Francisco, CA: Berrett-Koehler.

Costley, C., Elliott, G. and Gibbs, P. (2010) *Doing Work-Based Research: Approaches to Enquiry for Insider Researchers*. London: Sage.

Crotty, M. (1998) *The Foundations of Social Research: Meaning and Perspective in the Research Process*. London: Sage.

Cullen, J., Hedges, H. and Bone, J. (2011) Planning, undertaking and disseminating research, in S. Callan and M. Reed (eds), *Work-Based Research in the Early Years*. London: Sage. pp. 121–34.

Denscombe, M. (2010) *The Good Research Guide: For Small-Scale Social Research Projects*. 4th edn. Buckingham: Open University Press.

Denzin, N.K. (2006) *Sociological Methods: A Sourcebook*. Chicago, IL: Aldine Transaction.

Denzin, N.K. and Lincoln, Y. (eds) (2003) *The Landscape of Qualitative Research: Theories and Issues*. 2nd edn. London: Sage.

Department for Children, Schools and Families (DCSF) (2003) *The Every Child Matters Agenda*. London: HMSO.

Department for Children, Schools and Families (DCSF) (2008) *Statutory Framework for the Early Years Foundation Stage*. Nottingham: DCSF.

Department for Education (DfE) (2012) *Statutory Framework for Early Years Foundation Stage (EYFS)*. London: The Stationery Office.

Dockett, S., Einarsdottir, J. and Perry, B. (2009) Researching with children: ethical tensions, *Early Childhood Research*, 7(3): 283–98.

Early Childhood Australia Inc. (2010) *The Code of Ethics*. Online at: http://www.earlychildhoodaustralia.org.au/code_of_ethics/early_childhood_australias_code_of_ethics.html#top (accessed 3 March 2012).

Ely, M. (1991) *Doing Qualitative Research: Circles within Circles*. London: Falmer Press.

Fetterman, D. (2010) *Ethnography: Step-by Step*. 3rd edn. London: Sage.

Fleer, P. and Barker, A. (2008) An instructional approach for improving the writing of literature reviews, *Journal of Music Teacher Education*, 17: 69–82.

Flewett, R. (2005) Conducting research with young children: some ethical considerations, *Early Childhood Development and Care*, 175(6): 553–65.

Flick, U. (2011) *Introducing Research Methodology. A Beginner's Guide to Doing a Research Project*. London: Sage.

Floyd, A. and Linet, A. (2010) Researching from within: ethical and moral dilemmas, paper at Oxford Brookes University. Online at: www.srhe.ac.uk/conference2010/abstracts/0108.pdf (accessed 17 October 2013).

Formosinho, J. and Formosinho, O. (2012) Towards a social science of the social: the contribution of praxeological research, *European Early Childhood Education Research Journal*, 20(4): 591–606.

Glaser, B.G. (1992) *Basics of Grounded Theory and Analysis*. Mill Valley, CA: Sociology Press.

Glesne, C. and Peshkin, A. (1992) *Becoming Qualitative Researchers: An Introduction*. White Plains, NY: Longman.

Hammersley, M. and Atkinson, P. (1983) *Ethnography: Principles in Practice*, London: Tavistock.

Harcourt, D., Perry, B. and Waller, T. (2011) *Researching Young Children's Perspectives*. Oxford: Routledge.

Hart, C. (2001) *Doing a Literature Search – a Comprehensive Guide for the Social Sciences*. London: Sage.

Hase, S. and Kenyon, C. (2000) *From Andragogy to Heutagogy*. Melbourne: ultiBASE.

Havercamp, B. and Young, R.A. (2007) Paradigms, purpose and the role of literature: formulating a rationale for qualitative investigations, *The Counselling Psychologist*, 35: 265–94.

Jacobson, W. (1998) Defining the quality of practitioner research, *Adult Education Quarterly*, 48: 125–38.

James, A. (2007) Ethnography in the study of children and childhood, in P. Atkinson, A. Coffey, S. Delamont, J. Loftland and L. Loftland (eds), *Handbook of Ethnography*. London: Sage. pp. 246–57.

James, D. (2004) *Inquiry in Practice: Experiences, Insights and Interventions*. London: LSDA.

Jesson, J.K., Matheson, L. and Lacey, F.M. (2011) *Doing Your Literature Review*. London: Sage.

Lambert, V. and Glacken, M. (2011) Engaging with children in research: theoretical and practical implications of negotiating informed consent/assent, *Nursing Ethics*, 18: 781–801.

Le Gallais, T. (2004) Too busy reacting to reflect! A case study of a group of novice researchers involved in their first action research project set within an FE college in the West Midlands, paper presented at BERA Conference, UMIST, 16–18 September. Online at: www.leeds.ac.uk/educol/documents/00003718.doc (accessed 20 October 2012).

Luca, M. (2009) Embodied research and grounded theory. University of Wales, UK. Online at: http://www.wales.ac.uk/en/featuredcontent/articles/staffarticles/EmbodiedResearchandGroundedTheory.aspx.(accessed 13 February 2012).

MacNaughton, G. (2004) Exploring critical constructive perspectives on children's learning, in A. Anning, J. Cullen and M. Fleer (eds), *Early Childhood Education: Society and Culture*. London: Sage.

MacNaughton, G., Rolfe, S.A. and Siraj-Blatchford, I. (2001) *Doing Early Childhood Research*. Buckingham: Open University Press.

McDowall Clark, R. (2012) I've never thought of myself as a leader but…: the early years professional and catalytic leadership. *European Early Childhood Education Research Journal*, 20(3): 391–401.

McNiff, J. (2010) *Action Research for Professional Development*. Poole: September Books.

McNiff, J. (2011) Where the wonderful things are: a celebration of global interconnectedness for professional accountability through action research, paper presented at the Value and Virtue in Practice-Based Research Conference, York St John University, 1–2 June.

McNiff, J. and Whitehead, J. (2010) *Doing and Writing Action Research*. London: Sage.

McNiff, J. and Whitehead, J. (2011) *All You Need to Know About Action Research*. 2nd edn. London: Sage.

Moustakas, C. (1994) *Phenomenological Research Methods*. Thousand Oaks, CA: Sage.

Mukherji, P. and Albon, D. (2010) *Research Methods in Early Education. An Introductory Guide*. London: Sage.

New Zealand Association for Inquiry in Education (1998) *Ethical Guidelines*. Online at: http://www.nzare.org.nz/pdfs/NZAREEthical Guidelines2010.pdf. (accessed 3 August 2012).

Nolan, A., Macfarlane, K. and Cartmel, J. (2013) *Research in Early Childhood*. London: Sage.

Norton, L. (2009) *Action Research in Teaching and Learning*. Oxford: Routledge.

Papatheodorou, T., Luff, P. and Gill, J. (2011) *Child Observation for Learning and Research*. Harlow: Pearson.

Pascal, C. (2012) Bringing research to life, unpublished conference proceedings, BECERA Conference, Midlands Arts Centre, Birmingham, 15–16 February.

Pascal, C. and Bertram, T. (2012a) Praxeological research within a learning community: developing evidence based practice, keynote presentation to the British Early Education Research Association (BERA) Conference, Birmingham, 4–6 September.

Pascal, C. and Bertram, T. (2012b) Praxis, ethics and power: developing praxeology as a participatory paradigm for early childhood research, *European Early Childhood Education Research Journal*, 20(4): 477–92.

Pascal, C. and Bertram, T. (2012c) Praxis, ethics and power: developing praxeology as a participatory paradigm for early childhood research, paper presented at the 22nd EECERA Conference, Porto, Portugal, 1 September.

Pring, R. (2004) *Philosophy of Education: Aims, Theory, Common Sense and Research*. London: Continuum.

Punch, S. (2002) Research with children: the same or different as research with adults?, *Childhood*, 9: 321–41.

Radnor, H. (2002) *Researching Your Professional Practice*. Buckingham: Open University Press.

Rawlings, A. (2008) *Studying Early Years: A Guide to Work Based Learning*. Maidenhead: Open University Press.

Reed, M. (2013) Practice based inquiry: a workshop, FdA Student Partner Conference, University of Worcester, 2 March.

Reed, M. and Canning, N. (eds) (2012) *Implementing Quality Improvement and Change in the Early Years*. London: Sage.

Reed, M and Walker, R. (2012) Early childhood practitioners developing an academic voice and tutors making sense of the research process, *NZ Research in Early Childhood Education Journal*, 15: 137–49. Online at: http://www.childforum.com/research/research-journal-articles-reviewed-ece/2012-nzrece-journal-articles/890-early-childhood-practitioners-practice-based-research-publish.html#ixzz2JyQBHHDg. (accessed 6 December 2012).

Richardson, L. (1998) Writing: a method of inquiry, in N.K. Denzin and Y.S. Lincoln (eds), *Collecting and Interpreting Qualitative Materials*. London: Sage. pp. 345–71.

Rike, C. and Sharp, L.K. (2008) Assessing pre-service teachers' dispositions: a critical dimension of professional preparation, *Childhood Education*, 84(3): 150–3.

Rinaldi, C. (2005) *In Dialogue with Reggio Emilia*. London: RoutledgeFalmer.

Roberts-Holmes, G. (2011) *Doing Your Early Years Research Project*. 2nd edn. London: Sage.

Scottish Educational Inquiry Association (SERA) (2005) *Ethical Guidelines for Educational Inquiry*. Online at: http://www.sera.ac.uk. (accessed 3 July 2012).

Silverman, D. (2000) *Doing Qualitative Research: A Practical Handbook*. London: Sage.

Smith, S. with Reed, M. and Callan, S. (2011) Identifying what has been found – explaining a new position, in S. Callan and M. Reed (eds), *Work-Based Research in the Early Years*. London: Sage. pp. 95–106.

Solvason, C. (2010) *Research and the Early Years Practitioner-Researcher*. Tactyc. Online at: www.tactyc.org.uk/pdfs/Reflection-Solvason.pdf. (accessed 12 April 2012).

Solvason, C. (2011) Expressing personal values and beliefs – the essential position of the researcher, in S. Callan and M. Reed (eds), *Work-Based Research in the Early Years*. London: Sage. pp. 32–44.

Spradley, J. P. (1979) *The Ethnographic Interview*. New York: Holt, Rinehart and Winston.

Stake, R.E. (1995) *The Art of Case Study Research*. Thousand Oaks, CA: Sage.

Stern, J. (2011) From negative ethics to positive virtues in inquiry, paper presented at the Value and Virtue in Practice-Based Research Conference, York St John University, 1–2 June.

Sylva, K., Melhuish, E.C., Sammons, P., Siraj-Blatchford, I. and Taggart, B. (2004), *The Effective Provision of Pre-School Education (EPPE) Project: Technical Paper 12 – The Final Report: Effective Pre-School Education*. London: DfES/Institute of Education, University of London.

Tirado, F. and Galvez, A. (2007) Positioning theory and discourse analysis: some tools for social interaction analysis, *Forum: Qualitative Social Research*, 8(2): art. 31.

Torraco, R. (2005) Writing integrative literature reviews: guidelines and examples, *Human Resource Development Review*, 4: 356–67. Online at: http://hrd.sagepub.com/content/4/3/356 (accessed 16 July 2012).

Tummers, L. and Karsten, N. (2011) Reflecting on the role of literature in qualitative public administration research: learning from grounded theory, *Administration and Society*, 44(1): 64.

Walsham, G. (2006) Doing interpretive research, *European Journal of Information Systems*, 15: 320–30.

Walter, I., Nutley, S. and Davies, H. (2005) What works to promote evidence-based practice? A cross sector review, *Evidence and Policy*, 1: 33–63.

Wenger, E. (1998) *Communities of Practice: Learning, Meaning and Identity*. Cambridge: Cambridge University Press.

Wenger, E. (2010) Landscapes of Practice, a series of workshops held at the Practice-based Professional Learning Centre for Excellence in Teaching and Learning, Open University. Online at: http://www8.open.ac.uk/opencetl/resources/pbpl-resources/etienne-wenger. (accessed 20 November 2010).

Wenger, E., McDermott, R. and Snyder, W. (2002) *Cultivating Communities of Practice*. Boston, MA: Harvard Business School Press.

Index

Added to a page number 'f' denotes a figure and 't' denotes a table.